A *Vineyard* *Year*

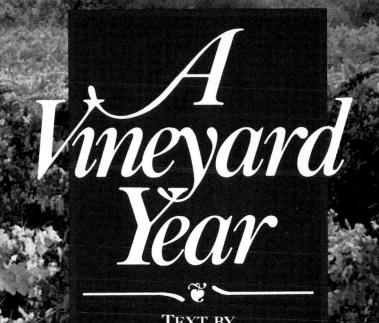

A Vineyard Year

TEXT BY
JOSEPH NOVITSKI

PHOTOGRAPHS BY
NICK PAVLOFF

CHRONICLE BOOKS
San Francisco

To Cathy and Paula,
who said, "Why don't you guys write a book?"

ACKNOWLEDGMENTS

The author would like to acknowledge his debt to his immediate neighbors, Richard Mounts, Allan Nelson, and Americo Rafanelli, without whose assistance and advice he never would have made it through his first vineyard year, and this book could not have been written. From that first year onward, many others helped him learn enough to make his own farming mistakes, including Ronald Black; Siri and Rick Buchignani; Eugene Cuneo; Bill Frost; Fred, Joe, and Don Guadagni; Howard Hare and his late father; John Naber; Carl Petersen; Dane Petersen; Jerry Petersen; Terry Proschold; David Rafanelli; Richard Rued; Bernie Steindorf; Wayne Steindorf; Mike and Frank Teldeschi and their sons, Ray, Gary, Dan, and John; Joe Vogensen and Alex Vyborny. None of these men is responsible for the contents of this book, but without the knowledge they, and so many others from West Dry Creek to St. Helena, shared so freely, it would not have been possible.

Author and photographer join in thanking the staff of the Wine Institute in San Francisco for much speedy research assistance. We would also like to thank Bob Keeble and his whole staff at Frei Brothers Winery, Healdsburg, California, for several years of kindness and hospitality while we worked on this project, and Bob Atkinson, managing winemaker at the Stony Ridge Winery, Pleasanton, California. Finally, we both owe a large debt to Bill LeBlond, who let us crawl over his transom at Chronicle Books, and with him to Larry Smith. Both supplied the concrete encouragement that saw the project through. The author would like to add thanks to Linda Gunnarson, who had a surer eye for his style than he, and, as editor, made it hold throughout.

LIBRARY OF CONGRESS CATALOGING IN PUBLICATION DATA
NOVITSKI, JOSEPH
A VINEYARD YEAR.
INCLUDES INDEX.
1. VITICULTURE—CALIFORNIA—DRY CREEK VALLEY (SONOMA COUNTY)
2. WINE AND WINE MAKING—CALIFORNIA—DRY CREEK VALLEY (SONOMA COUNTY)
I. PAVLOFF, NICK. II. TITLE.
SB387.76.C2N68 1983 634.8'09794'18 83-14445
ISBN 0-87701-282-2

EDITED BY LINDA GUNNARSON

Chronicle Books
870 MARKET STREET
SAN FRANCISCO, CALIFORNIA 94102

Contents

Serenity in the summer
vineyard, after the spring rush.

This book will not teach those who want to become grape growers and winemakers how to do so. In fact, as experienced growers will quickly notice, the text is not technically exhaustive at all. For example, any grape grower with one full season of experience will see by the second chapter that the author is pruning only head-trained, spur-pruned vines and nowhere describes how to bring out a cordon or how many Cabernet canes to leave in a trellised North Coast vineyard. However, the author hopes that all growers will recognize some of the decisions they face every year and how they feel as they take nature's choices and make their own.

The book was written and photographed for those who do not grow wine grapes for a living as a story of where wines come from and why they are "heavy," or "thin," or "fruity," or "full-bodied," or any other of those things that wine writers have described in many excellent books. This book is a recounting of how many days, of what kinds go together to make "a good year" for wine in northern California.

To those who still yearn to be viticulturalists after reading *A Vineyard Year,* the author suggests the standard text on the business of grape growing: *General Viticulture* by A.J. Winkler, et al.; University of California Press; Berkeley, 1962. The author would also venture to recommend that any prospective vineyardist make certain he can afford to go farming.

CHAPTER ONE

The Romance of Farming

There are winter days when a healthy vineyard looks like the fading photograph of some World War I battlefield. No colors are left but the washed-out brown in a few tattered leaves. Vines march away in rows, black and brittle, into a mist that flows up and hides the horizon. The wet ground seems frozen in ungainly grey heaves, and no reminder is left of the green exuberance with which the vines grew through the spent summer or the whirling excitement of harvest just completed. The faint fresh smell of growing vines and the little rustling noises they make to themselves are gone, and so are the tastes and smells of the growing season: turned earth and dust, diesel fuel and sulfur and, finally, the slightly oversweet taste of ripe grapes waiting their turn at a winery.

Such a dull and frozen day seems a very unpromising time to begin anything to do with growing; yet pruning is the most important single thing a grape grower does in a vineyard, and pruning should best begin on a day like that. During each growing season, time flows through a vineyard like a familiar river. Event rushes onto expected event in a sequence that is known, but unstopping and unstoppable.

The life of every year sweeps like a current from budbreak each spring, through growth and ripening, to harvest; sometimes racing and tumbling, sometimes slowing, spreading, even eddying back, but always carrying the grape grower along, ready or not. At pruning time, in the dormant season, it is as though that river had frozen. Nothing moves. The grower can climb out, as it were, stand back and figure out the best way to take next year's rush. No pressing hurry, no distraction gets in the way of the internal imagining that tells each grower and those who prune with him that a vine will grow so, in the year to come, and that the crop will best form from these buds on this cane, not

Sunlit buds after a light spring rain.

A vineyard in autumn: any
visitor to the wine country
sees the beautiful colors, while
a grape grower knows that red
leaves are the symptom of an
incurable disease.

those on that one. For weeks or months beginning on such a dull and frozen day, the cuts made in the bare, brown canes that stand in a tangled arch above each vine will determine, more than anything else, how much crop and of what quality will grow and, God willing, become wine on some warm afternoon next autumn.

Pruning, like much of farming, is an act of faith. The men deciding what wood to leave and what to cut away have no guarantee that there will be enough water to carry the crop they are beginning to build through the summer, or enough sun to get it ripe in the fall. They cannot guess whether the growing season will be long and even or full of fits, starts and restarts brought on by extremes in the weather. Sometimes, in fact, it hardly seems likely to the pruner that the stumpy little tree before him, with its bark hanging in long, brown tatters and last year's growth, in dormancy, showing all the scars from its fights with whatever insect or fungus was the worst enemy last year, will ever grow wine grapes again. However, it has happened before and it should happen again; so a man gets on with his pruning.

Pruning can begin any time after the first hard frost knocks the leaves off the vines. Here, in the Dry Creek Valley, sixty miles northwest of San Francisco and twenty-six miles east as a high-altitude crow might fly over four forested ridges from the Pacific Ocean, the ready signal might come on a hard, white morning in late October or November. It might come in a drenching November fog or with the cold, dry wind that rakes through our vineyards after the first storm from the Gulf of Alaska.

In this valley, if the signal comes early, most farmers ignore it for a while. The frantic days of harvest may only be a month gone, there may still be cleaning up and equipment mending to do and it is good to coast a bit, savoring the warmth from a new wood stove perhaps and pretending to work at getting the accounts ready for tax time.

Putting things off is usually well outside our local code of behavior; however, even procrastination may not seem dishonorable when a grower knows that what he must do next means making his best guess about the future, then

cutting up his vines to fit his vision. But one day one grower starts, then another, and by early January we all will have decided to get on with it.

"Getting on with it" is the human rhythm of farming, and this book, for all the beauty of vineyards and the stirrings of the soul from good wines, is about farming. It is the story of one year in a wine grape vineyard that might be a year in any vineyard. The story is about wine grapes, the vines that grow them and how growers tend those vines in a small region of northern California that is best known for its Zinfandel wines. The year, 1980, was pronounced "good," on balance, by some experts, and its story should tell how many hours and days, and of what kinds, make a good year for wine.

Wines begin with dirt farming. There is magic enough in ordinary farming, to be sure, but no tangible romance of the kind a visitor to wine country almost always seems to see, as, for example, when he catches sight of a farmer contemplating one flaming red vine in a sea of green and yellow leaves.

"Ah, what beautiful colors," the visitor will say.

"The reds were so lovely, we just had to stop," his wife will add. "You're very lucky to live here."

A man doesn't have the heart to tell them that the deep red leaves in that block of Zinfandel are a sure sign of incurable leafroll virus, which means 10 percent less production and one degree less sugar content at harvest for that vine for every harvest of its life.

There is beauty enough in farming to take the weariest eye by surprise, as on the morning after a winter rainstorm when the sun rises clear and low and turns every water drop on the arms of every bare vine into a tiny prism and the millions of flashing rainbows dance on for acres and acres. For that moment, there is beauty, but not of a kind to bring lasting tranquility into a farmer's life. There is magic, but it flows through the vines in a natural annual rhythm, not through grape farmers. Every year we watch and tend a miracle when the vines grow, ripen their grapes, then go to sleep again. A farmer's faith is in that magic, but his work

**Above: Time flows through
the vineyard year like
a familiar river.**

**Right: The romance of
farming. A grower and his
crew move a trailer-mounted
irrigation pump in the rain.**

goes on around it at whatever pace the yearly miracle sets. Coming in at the beginning, the middle or the end, a visitor may see the view; the farmer sees the work and lives with the magic, for better or for worse. It is simply a natural process. Sometimes it works for him; at times it does not.

In local usage, two separate meanings for the phrase "the romance of farming" have grown current since vineyard owners who did not grow up on tractors bought farms here in the wine boom of the early seventies. The two meanings illustrate the difference in point of view between the enchanted onlooker in wine country and the farmer who has to get in that country's cash crop. A lawyer, an oil man or a urologist may buy a hog farm, because hog farms have been good investments, and he may buy a vineyard. Over drinks or dinner, he who bought the hog farm will probably not talk about the thrill of farrowing a 320-pound Duroc sow, but he who bought the vineyard may well tell of the pruning or the picking at his country place, thus letting his listeners feel what some call the romance of farming.

In a farmer's vocabulary, that phrase has the taste of pure irony, and it is used in the shortest possible thrusts. Let us suppose that the heavy winter rains have apparently ended, the days are longer and the ground has dried somewhat and begun to warm. A grower's vines have begun to open their buds and push out leaves. In one or two days of work, hauling, fitting, testing, welding, retesting, adjusting and tightening, the grower has put his main pump back onto a stage cut low enough into the bank of Dry Creek so that winter's high water might flood it, but safe now that spring has arrived. He needs that pump badly to run his sprinklers for protection should a frost sneak in on some clear night. With the pump in place he is ready.

Three days later the wind goes round to the south and fills the mouth of the valley with black clouds, which sink lower and lower. Overnight, the skies open and two or three inches of rain fall. Perhaps the grower is fatalist enough to spare himself a walk through the plummeting rain at three in the morning to see how close the rising creek has come to his $11,000 pump, but just before dawn the roar of the little stream by the house tells him it's time to move.

Out of bed and down to the creek in the rain. Into the cold, brown water to unbind all the guy wires and pull the pump suction pipe out with chains and tractor. With the water still rising, unbolt and unhook the pump. Pull it up the streaming bank, blocking and rigging keeper chains every few feet so that if the tractor or the pump slip they won't both go into the creek. Done.

By midmorning the storm is over, bright patches are beginning to open in the sky and chase around the clouds and the grower is at the equipment dealer for parts to replace whatever it is he broke during the dawn scramble. So are his neighbors.

"Enough rain for you?" one will ask.

"Too much," another will answer, then ask, "Dry Creek come up much?"

"Five, maybe six feet," the grower will answer, with an attempt at dryness. "Had to pull my suction, then my pump."

"That high?" someone will say.

"Yes," he'll answer, and his indignation over nature's caprices will begin to swell inside. "And if the wind goes north today I'll have to do it all again tomorrow."

"That's the romance of farming," a man will say. His emphasis, the emphasis anyone here places on that phrase, draws out the *o* in *romance* so it is the longest, most tiring sound in the sentence.

One day, in the late fall or early winter, it's time to get on with pruning, and that is the romance of farming.

CHAPTER TWO

Pruning

Pruning established grapevines is a series of acres upon acres of individual production decisions: how much can this vine bear? How much should it bear to carry through a normal year, to pay the bills but sustain its quality? A grower and each of his pruners make roughly 200 such decisions every eight-hour working day from November or December through January and into February each year. Pruning for production is the foundation for all that a grape grower does for the rest of the year. Every act, every farming choice, builds on what is left on the mature vine after pruning.

Training young vines during the first three or four pruning seasons, before they are strong enough to carry a crop, is an undertaking with a different, longer view, extending the full life span of the vine, to fifteen or twenty-five, perhaps even fifty bearing years. The task is a little like teaching at a boarding school. In the first winter after planting, every one

A northern California coastal valley.

of the knee-high plants looks the same. A man will talk to each one and, in almost every case, cut it back to the ground to allow the root system to grow ahead of what is above the ground and form a sort of springboard from which the new vine will leap in the following summer. This first time through a new block, the grower is getting to know his vines and sensing how they will adapt to his soil. Grape growers generally call each separate, simultaneous planting of vines of one variety a "block," whether there arc one or one hundred acres in it. The main object in planting and training is to get all the young vines to bearing size and strength quickly, yet together.

By the second winter, the pruning teacher knows his pupils much better. Some, the standouts, have made it solidly to the top of the stake and are ready to be formed for the head or trellis, their adult shapes. Others, just as familiar now, are still lagging, unwilling to grow up just yet. Pruning them back again and giving

A pruner at work, cutting away last year's dormant growth and leaving next year's crop shaped on the vines behind him.

them special attention with individual waterings and fertilizer should help them catch up. Some few will not have made it, and although the teacher will know why, he will probably not be any less sad for knowing.

In their third winter, almost certainly, the new vines will have been trained to some uniformity. The uniformity, like that of any group of school graduates, is only in formal training. From now on, God, the ground and the nature and gifts of each vine will determine how fruitful it will be.

From the fourth year on, under normal circumstances, a pruning grower is no longer talking to each vine, but "listening," as it is called among some pruners, although what really is involved is a special vision, a way of watching a vine that comes with time on the job. The ideal pruner, with sharpened shears in his hand, steps up to a vine and opens his eyes. The vine will show him all he needs to know to begin cutting.

Do the canes grow out from the vine thicker than a man's thumb and trail ten feet or more onto the ground? That vine could do with more buds than it had to begin the growing season last year. Are the canes numerous but thin, standing almost straight out like the fingers of an emaciated hand? That vine probably had too much crop; so fewer buds might be best this year.

Most growers know their established blocks well enough to prune them so they will produce a crop that should get ripe enough to make good wine. Some go at it like drill sergeants: "Seven to nine two-bud spurs for Zinfandel on flat bottomland; five to seven on the hills." Others have less rigid formulations, but firm rules of thumb to guide each set of choices.

Which canes should a pruner choose to shape for next year's crop, from all that tangle sticking out of the vine's trunk and limbs, and which should he clip off the vine for good and leave for waste? The vine will show any pruner who has learned how to look at vines and understand what he sees. Understanding comes best and most easily from years of pruning along with older growers, in the comforting shade of their years of experience, but after a time every grower insists on making his own mistakes.

On any winter day, I make mine this way. There may be two canes growing from last year's spur, the stick of wood left after the previous winter's pruning, at the top of a vine. The canes that grew from that spur over the summer, at their best, are both smooth-skinned, round and straight. The buds push out at each joint in the cane. They are dark and wedge-shaped, almost like nascent talons; some point up and some point down. The spur we pruned last year has grown through the summer with the canes it pushed out, swelling its girth and beginning to split its once-smooth skin into bark. Which of the two canes will do that well again in the next growing season?

Generations of pruners have learned from generations of vines that the cane closest to last year's now-mature wood will be the most fruitful. So the ideal pruner counts two buds up from the root of that cane, allows a finger's width beyond and cuts. There is next year's spur, looking like a little wooden horn only two to three inches long.

At the next spur, there may be three canes. Two, the closest to the trunk, are flat and irregular-looking. They may be in the best position, but they do not look as round as the straight cane farthest from the trunk. Another lesson of generations comes to mind: flat canes grew in the shade, round canes in the sun. Sunlight makes fruitfulness; so make the round cane next year's spur and cut away its flat neighbors.

Pruning old vines or new, fancy varietals with canes that must be left just so long and tied back to trellis wires or the old Italian standbys that grow big, black bunches of fruit from spurs no longer or thicker than a healthy thumb, the rules are subtle, but simple and generically the same. Point the buds out and up, away from each other and into the sun. Count and clip. Make the keeping cuts first. Clip and saw and pull away the rest. Leave the vine standing bare, clean and ready, and wish it luck. Move on to the next. And "listen."

The pruner's work is a blend of rote and concentration, and his skill sharpens with repetition. His time at work and the work pace are circumscribed by nature. Both start when the vine leaves fall and end when growth begins again in March. By the nature of the work, also, starting each year is slow, hesitant, even a little painful.

"Friday, November 30. Clear. Warm," reads the entry in my field log for the day we began pruning for the 1980 crop. "0900–1700 Prune N. Gamay."

Napa Gamay vines grow large bunches of fleshy berries full of juice. On the vine or in the picker's bucket late in the year, their purple-blue skin, misted slightly by a bloom of silvery dust, makes Napa Gamay grapes an advertising artist's conception of how red-wine grapes should look.

Large, twisting canes, another family trait, make Gamay not a particularly friendly vine to prune. However, on that warm Friday in November, we needed to get on with the Gamay. The ten acres where it grows in the broad wedge between two paved county roads needed an application of lime, and the vines had to be pruned out of the way of the lime spreader before that work could begin.

Around the Dry Creek Valley, the rule of thumb inherited from the days before Prohibition, when the valley's vineyards were each the work of one family, is that one man can handily prune twenty acres, by himself, each winter. More than twenty acres becomes burdensome. By that rule, in a normal winter, four men could work steadily, pruning their way through our eighty acres. On the thirtieth, I began with Miguel and Juan Silva, brothers who had worked one season with me already. I knew their work and trusted it. Roberto Martinez and Baltazar Gonzalez had asked to prune, and they were starting for the first time that day. All were going to prune with hand shears and saws only, because it is my prejudice that hand shears make a man look more closely at the cut he is about to make, if only to be sure his thumb is not in the way. There is no danger to thumbs but perhaps some danger of inattention to the vines when a hired pruner uses long-handled lopping shears.

The sun had been out for half an hour by the time I had finished explaining that I wanted no limbs below the knee, two buds on every spur and the same number of spurs as last year. Working and explaining as I cut and cleared and cut again, I pruned eight or ten vines into the first row. I stopped to watch each of the men in turn as he did a vine in the same row.

Miguel and Juan were impatient to start on their own. Roberto showed that he knew what a pruned vine should look like. By ten, each was working in his own row of vines. The short, dry snipping sounds of each cut were beginning to blend into a steady stream, with fewer pauses for consideration. I walked behind the slowly advancing front, watching, and pruning every second vine in Baltazar's row to keep him level with the others.

Baltazar is a cheery young man with a wide face set directly on a short barrel chest. He has a loud voice and large, protruding eyes. Digging and pouring a house foundation in close quarters in the heat of August earlier that year, he had been a steady, willing working companion. Pruning, now, was not so easy for him. The canes seemed to trap him so that he had to grasp each one in turn to cut it, then bob his head as he counted each bud. A right-handed pruner gathers the severed canes in his left hand as he goes, dropping them in the avenue between rows when he has a handful and keeping his field of vision clear. The focus of that field is two buds tall, and the other buds on a cane don't count. By midmorning, Baltazar had not learned the blank-minded trick of that focus, or caught the rhythm that makes pruning many vines each day possible. I had stopped trying to explain as I demonstrated. His face grew red each time I talked.

He ate lunch in silence, sitting alone in the shadow cast by a bare apple tree's trunk. The others came back from lunch laughing, in a low, blue car with loud dual exhausts. Their pace picked up in the afternoon. I could see that the brothers, Miguel and Juan, had remembered how to slide their hands back to the tips of the shear handles for more leverage to cut through thicker canes. Roberto was learning the trick from them. Baltazar, his right hand as tired as ours after four hours of unaccustomed squeezing, grasped the one-handed shears in his two fists and grunted when he attacked a fat cane.

By the end of that first day, Baltazar was rocking the shears around tough canes with two hands, making ragged cuts that heal slowly and are thus more open to fungus infection. The others, like me, were stopping every few vines to stretch their right hands. I had flat blisters nestled into the first joints of my middle and third fingers, the bearing surfaces for the shears.

"Fog. Saturday, December 1. 0800–1700 Miguel, Juan, Roberto, Baltazar, Gabriel prune Gamay," reads the next field log entry.

One of the advantages to starting early and in a block of vines by a paved road is that the word you have begun work gets around quickly to potential employees who may have been idle since harvest. Most hiring here is done at the roadside, the negotiations carried out in Spanish over the faded hood of an Impala, or a Fairlane or a Camaro now several years out of date. Rarely does someone frankly volunteer to help, as did Gabriel Torres, who was the driver and proud owner of the loud, low, blue car. A lithe, quick youth with black curling hair and a very white smile, Gabriel had quit his job in quality control at the end of an electronic equipment assembly line down county in order to prune through the winter as part of a team, for hire to growers as one unit, with his father and brothers. He said he liked pruning much better than squinting all day through a magnifying glass the size of his face, even though it meant half the money and much colder feet. It was my luck that his father had not yet started pruning for the growers who had already reserved the Torres team for the winter, because Gabriel was a natural, and he wanted to warm up with his friends while waiting.

Gabriel moved smoothly and made sure cuts. Sometimes he talked—of friends and women, dances here and the news from Mexico—and sometimes he did not. We all began to move at his pace, as long as I was able to prune often in Baltazar's row to keep him abreast of the rest. That pace was steady and it increased steadily. By the end of the day we had done 150 vines each, respectable enough for the second day out but not productive enough to make economic sense all winter.

"Perhaps, if I took the row next to Baltazar, I could show him," Gabriel suggested after lunch. We were talking over the hood of his car, at his request, and I noticed that the chrome clip pins that held the hood down and the pierced chrome pins they clipped into were carefully polished.

"Fine. Good idea."

"Perhaps you would tell the others it's all right to listen to me?"

I did, and the work appeared to slow. That weekend I was left with a sore hand that curled into a claw when I slept, and doubts about Baltazar. On Monday the weather turned slowly cloudier and colder, and I found other things to do in order to leave the crew largely alone.

It was a deliberate test. It seems to turn out that when a pruning crew is fairly well balanced and all know what to do, the best man sets the pace and the work goes well. When one or two are less skilled or less gifted than the others, pruning slows. The better, or older, men in the crew almost invariably leave their own rows to help the slowest keep up, and the advancing front of pruned vines stays even but moves more slowly. The slowest man, in this case of imbalance, sets the pace for all.

In the dark twilight of Monday afternoon I counted 120 vines per man pruned in the day and knew that Baltazar would never make a vine pruner. All were slowing to his pace. I found it so embarrassing to fire him that I waited a day or more until I found another grower who was hiring men and women to tie pruned vines back onto his wire trellises. Baltazar's willingness to work fit well with the other farmer, and his leaving felt more like a transfer than a dismissal.

A pruned vine sleeps.

Above: A spider's winter web, snugged down into the crotch of a mature grapevine.

Right: Wild mustard begins to bloom well into the winter pruning season, as the days grow longer and Pacific storms grow warmer.

"Frost. Friday, December 7. 0730–1630 prune Gamay. Finish. Paid all."

By then, all four of the remaining pruners were finishing 200 vines or more per day. They proved it to me when I worked all Friday afternoon with them, taking a row of my own. Toward the end of the afternoon, with the sun still out but losing its warmth as it lowered, they moved away from me so steadily that the snipping rhythm and their slow chatting faded almost out of hearing. The wind from the south whispered instead, and a red-shoulder hawk worked a slow spiral over the vineyard, looking for supper. I heard the wind in his pinions before I looked up. The crew turned back at the end of their rows and quickly pruned back up my row toward me, smiling and occasionally laughing as they drew closer.

It was a display, of course, of their rediscovered skill and speed. We wound up the day with it and it made us all feel good. They had shown me how well they could prune and nailed down their claims for a full winter's work. I was pleased and could even show a little chagrin over how much quicker than me they had become, because they had taught me something else about pruning.

There is a Spanish saying that the best fertilizer is the owner's footprint. The best pruning pace, it seems, comes on the day the owner prunes along with his crew.

Friday's frost and the hawk sensed before I had seen him were reassuring also. A few days of hard frost early in the winter, with fairly regular freezes thereafter, put the vines thoroughly to sleep. There are fancy phrases for it, but the rest that comes with cold is a real vineyard need. Without it, vine growth may break early and move swiftly, but often it is almost febrile, overextended and more subject to disease. The crop appears thinner and the wines made from it taste thin.

Sensing the hawk meant that the pruning mood was back. Pruning is repetitious work, but it requires concentration. Seeing the same thing over and over and doing the same things again and again can scatter one's concentration.

Or that repetition can bring on a mood that is almost meditative.

At its best, that mood works so that a pruner sees the vine and understands it, begins cutting and then also sees other things: the walnut shell halves at the foot of a vine, which mean a crow stopped on that stake to crack open a meal last fall; the sodden little hollow of grasses in a crotch against a vine stake, left behind after a small bird, a finch or titmouse perhaps, raised a family in that vine last summer. There are gopher trails near the surface of the wet ground and occasional wobbly young field mice trying their legs in the new grass. There are spiders moving slowly in their winter quarters under strands of bark against the vine trunks. Such small, slow scenes are scarce and not distracting. In general, the pruning mood fits the winter season well, and the spareness of that slow season fits the pruner's need for concentration.

The dormant season is a contemplative time of year for grape growing. A farmer feels fairly flush with the proceeds of last year's harvest—at least flush enough so that the facts of his life, that payday comes only once a year while the bills come monthly, seem not to pinch so hard as they will later. Nothing is overwhelmingly pressing in the way that so many things are when growth is on and clamoring for attention.

The weather helps to bend a grower's attention to pruning, winter's central task, as the days darken and the year seems to slow down. There are fogs that clear slowly and fogs that cling all day with a cold insistence that eventually works inside the warmest clothes. There are frosts hard enough to sting a pruner's fingers each time he grasps a cane, even in full sunlight two hours after dawn. Overcasts move in from the Pacific Ocean like huge grey wedges, steadily pressing the horizon down from the redwoods on the hills to the bare oak tops in the valley. After the storms that follow these overcasts inland, there is mud in each row that can cling to rubber boots so hard it is occasionally necessary to step out of one of them to pull it free. All of this

—the cold, the fogs, the dark grey overcasts and the wet ground—turn a pruner's gaze down and in, to each vine and the work at hand.

Only on days after a warmer storm than most, a Hawaiian storm that leaves the sky washed like a clean, blue china bowl overhead and pulls after it a bustling northwest wind that ruffles the blue reflection of the sky in every puddle and tosses the wet grass like ocean waves, is a pruner tempted to look up. The robins and cedar waxwings, he finds, are moving about and talking impolitely to one another. The dogs are chasing a jackrabbit they will never catch. The yellow bursts of wild mustard blooms wave above new grass so deeply green it is almost blue, and a pruner may notice with surprise how tall both have grown since his work began. The noticing is reassuring in itself. Surprise, on such a warm, blue day means that concentration is upon him and holding.

For a grower who does some pruning himself, this contemplative winter work is like a series of visits to hospital patients. Pruning season is the only time of the year he looks closely at each vine in turn, seeing the marks of disease or malnutrition and noting the need for a stake here, new ties there or a new vine where the tractor, in a moment of carelessness, bit off an old vine at the ground. The medical history of the past year is more clearly apparent then, and what to do about it comes more readily to an uncluttered mind. The whole vineyard is full of history and promise.

Late in the 1980 pruning season, I started major surgery on all the vines in a twelve-acre block of Carignane, a red grape that makes the country red wines of southwestern France and, in California, supplies the bones, the blush and the sinews of many, many burgundies. The vines grow well and bear heavily, and thence sprang the problem that could be cured only by surgery. My Carignane vines, planted and trained by a predecessor facing a less demanding group of winemakers than have recently come to work in this corner of California, had grown through fourteen years into three

tiers. The topmost branches grew splendid canes into the sun, and the next staggered limbs down the five-foot trunks stretched well into the rows to reach what sunlight was left; but the lowest branches lived, worked and grew fruit in the shade. As a result, while grapes on the upper two-thirds of the vines could ripen in time to become wine, the shaded bottom third never had a chance, and grapes growing there could remain sour enough at harvest time to make a wine-maker's teeth creak.

For uniformity, for quality and for my peace of mind at harvest, the lowest limbs had to come off. I went at the job, early in February, with a small chainsaw buzzing in my hand and my heart in my mouth. Tearing off productive, living parts of vines that are my livelihood and leaving round, white scars running with sap did not come easily. I panted and fumbled so badly on the first day that I gashed a palm with the chainsaw. My field log entry is bleak.

"February 4. Pruning low limbs N. end Carign.," it reads. Thereafter a pencil line so sharp that it indents the paper stretches through the week, underlining the tense frustration of the job. However, by February 7, my usual weather observations expand again to fill the little daily blocks. I had worked out a technique for the stoop labor and had learned from the vines not only their life stories but the recent agricultural history of the valley.

The limbs that needed amputation were all well below my knee, sometimes as little as two hand spans off the ground. My predecessor on this farm, a cattleman by calling and bean grower by trade, had been feeling his way with a new crop on the soil where the Carignane grew. He had wanted production early, so the lowest limbs were trained out to bear fruit a scant year or two after planting. The Italians from around Lucca who brought wine grapes to this valley had always grown them on benchland, where the soil is shallow. Because vines did not grow vigorously in such soil and because this was the way vines were trained in Italy, all their vineyards, the models for the valley, were kept low. But my predecessor, sensing the advent of the wine boom that would soon push out his beans as well as prunes, apples and pears, had planted his Carignane on deep, strong, river-bottom soils late in the 1960s. The vines kept growing beyond the traditional hillside height. He tried again to head them out, one could see, at waist height, and still the Carignane wanted to grow more limbs and carry more crop. So there was a third spread of trained-out limbs on top, almost at the height of a man's shoulder.

Three tiers worked well for the farmer who planted and trained the Carignane block on the river-bottom soils. New wineries were opening when it began to bear, and old wineries were expanding. The demand for grapes was thirsty and not highly selective. In a year when the lowest Carignane limbs would not ripen their crop, an imaginative winemaker could make up for their lack of sugar in his fermenter. There are ways. But there are no Carignane-flavored additives or FDA-approved colors that match its purple, so my predecessor had sold his Carignane crops, even when they fell short of ideal sugar levels. My buyers, in a better-established market, could be more selective, and they were. As a result, I found myself that winter cutting down the bearing capacity of mature vines for the sake of quality. In the five previous seasons, other growers had been tearing out apple and pear trees, prune orchards and old vineyards to replace them all with new wine-grape vines whose names had been unfamiliar to most Americans ten years earlier. All of us were trying to catch up with the boom in wine drinking and to match the new American taste in wines.

Replanting to vineyards offered no guarantees of enduring success to any farmer. It was simply the necessary thing to do when the prices paid for apples, then for pears, fell below the cost of producing a crop. Wherever grapes had once grown well in Napa, Sonoma and Mendocino counties, California's established premium-wine country when the boom began, they were replanted and very quickly became the only crop that paid in parts of those three counties. Such wholesale changes are familiar in many farming regions, but the Dry Creek Valley had never before been so thoroughly committed to one crop as it was by the vineyard year of 1980.

"When I was a boy," a neighbor well into his thirties once told me, "there were small, family dairies making cream and butter under every bush out here.

"We had pears and prunes, too," he said. "We grew pole beans and ran turkeys on the hill one year, maybe pigs the next. After the hops moved to Oregon, my father said a man had to try a little bit of everything that would work, and we all did.

"Now there are grapes on every inch you can plant, and everybody will stay happy as long as the prices hold up. But they won't. They never do, once everyone catches on. Maybe there will be a new crop. More likely, we'll all end up planting houses."

His vision may prove right. The 1980 census found the fastest population increase in the San Francisco vicinity in our county, Sonoma, and it seems that more new houses go up on the hills above Dry Creek Valley every summer.

The lowest limbs on these vines were amputated to improve the quality of the grapes they will bear.

My winter surgery on the Carignane vines was not a bold step in any new direction, but rather a farmer's compromise, designed to keep that land in production while I waited, as all of us do, to see if consumers will go on wanting what grows there.

After two weeks in 1980, I stopped sawing, halfway through the block, to see what the next harvest would bring. With their cuts all healing under brown pruning seal, the trimmed vines looked almost lissome and ready to spring into growth, like a row of dancers poised at the barre. Their unsawn neighbors looked crabbed and frowzy, their lowest limbs like ragged skirts dragging in the mud.

At the following harvest the northern end of the block, after surgery, showed much better sugar content without any substantial drop in tonnage. I told Ray Teldeschi, an Italian farmer who represents the third generation of local grape growers in his family, and I may even have sounded proud.

"Vines," said Ray, "are very forgiving."

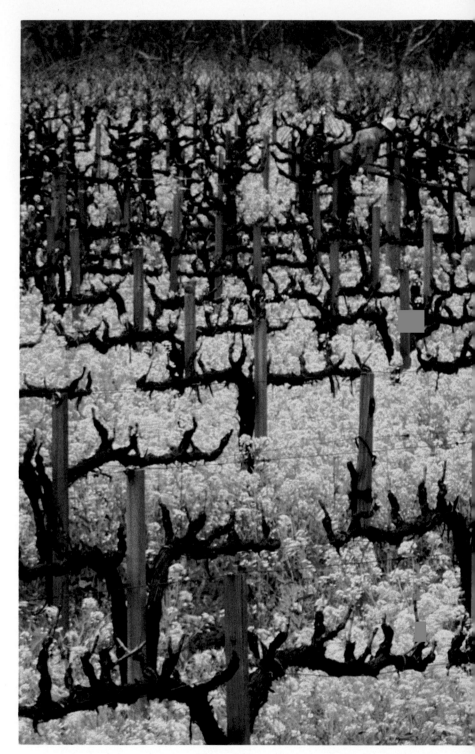

At the end of winter, with the wild mustard at the peak of bloom, grapevines stand pruned and ready for spring.

CHAPTER THREE

The Dry Creek Valley

Commercial wine-grape growing came to the Dry Creek Valley, as it did to all but a few of California's vineyard regions, with farming immigrants from northern Italy. They sought out California as a land of opportunity, leaving behind the pinched end of the last century, and brought their own tastes and farmer's judgments with them. Hereabouts, they worked at first as hired hands in the hopyards and orchards then covering the heavy, black soils in the alluvial plain of the Russian River, but they looked up shrewdly at the shallow soils on the hillsides and benches. Such land, they knew, made marvelous vineyards in the mountains north west of Florence, around Lucca, whence many of them had come.

When Italian immigrants could buy land, many bought the dry, scrub-covered hills on which established local farmers had turned their backs. In the climate of northern California, where almost six months of cold, drenching rains are followed by six months of dry growing weather, the same properties that made the hillsides next to useless in the established view shone full of promise for the farmers from northern Italy. The hillsides had shallow, less fertile soils? So much the better. Vines grown on such soils would not burden growers with extra growth and crops too heavy to manage.

The hillsides dried out in the first blast of summer heat, withering everything that grew on them, except deep-rooted, small trees, to a dry, lion-hide brown? So much the better. Cultivated grapevines are small trees whose roots go as deep as they can manage, and many of the wine grape varieties shaped by centuries of selection in Europe show signs of desert ancestry. They grow fast, early in the year, then concentrate on maturing their fruit. They scavenge hard for water and are tolerant of drought.

A Victorian farmhouse in the Dry Creek Valley.

The Italians who bought small farms of "worthless" ground in northern California beginning three generations ago knew that on shallow soils in hot, dry summers, shy-bearing vines turn their efforts inward and make grapes of very intense flavor, the best for making wine. Furthermore, heat that sears grasses and weeds means an end to cultivation and hoeing early in the year. To the new farmers, the withering heat meant that nothing would compete with well-rooted vines for moisture in the soil, and that mildew and rot, starved for humidity, should not thrive. Finally, the rivers and geological accidents that had shaped many of California's farming valleys had made what looked like a promised land to the Italian immigrants. On the benchland here, on flat steps of alluvial soil between valley floors and the foothills, it was as though miles of laboriously maintained Italian hillside terraces had been rolled out side by side into convenient acres of almost level ground.

So the first generation of Italian farming immigrants in the Dry Creek Valley, as in the huge San Joaquin Valley to the south and the Napa Valley immediately to the southeast, recovered the overlooked land and began growing grapes and making wine, often sold to other Italian immigrants living in nearby cities. Their tastes, their experience and their farming practices established the early pattern of commercial plantings and shaped this area. Their wines, made and blended according to traditional Italian country formulas, gave the next generations of Californians a taste for wine with food.

At the same time, the now-fashionable French-style vineyards and wineries got their nineteenth-century start in the Napa and Sonoma valleys and in the hills south and west of San Francisco. However, Italian-style wines, more or less dry, drinkable reds and whites sold to restaurants by the barrel, wines of the kind that sat on North Beach tables in San Francisco for the bohemians of the thirties and the beatniks of the fifties, were the foundation stones on which the mass market for California wines was eventually built.

The first farms here that were built around wine grapes as a cash crop were family affairs and therefore rather small. Twenty planted acres was the accepted outside limit one man might handle with his family and seasonal outside help. In the Dry Creek Valley, many vineyards started about the turn of the century were apparently that size or smaller, but they left their mark. One family winery up a canyon on the west side of the valley once dumped pressings, lees and juice into the creek at their door, enough so that the creek ran red at times, the old-timers say. The winery is gone, but the stream is still labeled Wine Creek on the United States Geological Survey's Geyserville Quadrangle map.

Outside the Napa Valley, it seems that only vineyards on a family scale survived the double blow of the Depression and Prohibition. There were reasons of scale built into the temperance law. Eugene Cuneo, whose family vineyard in Dry Creek Valley grew from 20 acres to almost 200 before he retired after the 1980 crop, remembers stacking wine grapes in forty-pound wooden boxes onto the splintered flat bed of the family farm's truck after each day's picking during Prohibition. His father drove 150 miles, to San Francisco and back, each night to sell wine grapes in the Italian neighborhoods of North Beach. Each head of a family was permitted, even during Prohibition, to make 200 gallons of wine for family consumption each year, and it takes at least one and a third tons of wine grapes to make 200 gallons of wine. The family market, supplied by family growers, flourished in the shade of the Eighteenth Amendment. Larger wineries sold juice or sacramental wine to the extent that they could and, where they could not, closed and converted their vineyards to orchards.

After Prohibition, the same pattern of family vineyards held here until after World War II had ended and then beyond. One of his neighbors in the San Joaquin Valley claims to remember seeing Julio Gallo, whose wine-producing empire is the largest in the world, driving his own truck loaded with grapes for crushing to a winery reopened after the Eighteenth Amendment was repealed. Gallo has come the longest way since then, perhaps, but every wine-grape-growing family in California has made huge technical leaps in one generation. At the very head of the Dry Creek

Valley lives a farmer of Scandinavian origin, now well into his seventies, who told me once with pride that he still pulls a set of plows through his vineyards with a tractor each spring, although it is a fading practice, because he always has.

"Of course," he said, "it used to take me and two teams of horses two dry weeks to plow forty acres. I changed teams in the middle of the day, and the horses and me, we only rested three times between sunup and sundown."

In recent springs, that farmer has plowed three times as much ground on each of his working days, riding a chattering green tractor. Meanwhile, his son and partner gets the tillage done on almost 150 acres in the same time the father and his horses once used on forty. All of us, whether our names are known around the world, like Gallo's, or only at the local auto parts store, now try to live up to the hyper-productive ideal of American commercial agriculture. In most cases, it is the only way to keep up with mortgage payments.

Well before the 1980 crop year, the two central ideas of American postwar productivity—large scale and appropriate technology—had settled into wine grape production. Marketing techniques had jostled and coddled the growing American taste for wine. And suddenly, for those outside looking on, there had been a boom in wine demand from 1970 to 1980. The prices paid for wine grapes rose to un-dreamed-of levels in those years and held high, so farmers in California, anywhere in California where grapes might remotely fit, planted vineyards. All over the state, vineyards came down from the hills, so to speak, in those ten years and changed from a specialty crop confined to certain regions to an industrial undertaking. Grapes of all kinds became California's second-ranking cash crop, by value, after cotton. Between 1970 and 1980, according to the United States Department of Agriculture technicians who survey California grape acreage every year, 223,113 new acres of wine varieties were planted, almost doubling the total acres of vineyards in the state.

In the same decade, professors of winemaking at the

Carl Petersen and his son and farming partner, Jerry, represent the second and third generations in their family to farm the head of the Dry Creek Valley.

Northern California's coastal
valleys, with sharp hills and
hummocky valley floors, catch
wine grapes' favorite climates
and coax the highest quality
out of grapevines.

University of California at Davis taught their students how to take apart the chemistry of wines and how, if nature granted half a chance, to put it back together again year after year with practically undetectable variations in taste. That consistency of taste is the only real requirement for a successful table wine, and as early as 1970 there were several successful California table wines sold from coast to coast.

The best marriage of industrial farming and wine-making by chemical rules in California was made in the San Joaquin Valley, the huge, hot slice of California farmland between Sacramento and Bakersfield, where the first successful mass-market table wines were put together and where most of them are still made. According to the Wine Institute, an industry-wide organization in San Francisco, three-quarters of all the wine grapes brought in for crushing in California in 1980 were grown on the flat, irrigated valley floor between those two cities.

The grapes are grown on land leveled by laser measurement and planted in rows laid out by surveying crews. Each vineyard row can be miles long. It often happens that thousands of acres are farmed by one manager, who has supervisors for each phase of the work in the vineyard year: one for cultivation, one for irrigation, one for spraying and dusting, each with his own new, radio-equipped pickup and his own crew of employees. Most of the men who oversee such vineyards are young and clean-shaven. They have short hair that is kept carefully cut under their polyester peaked caps, which advertise pesticides or tractors or banks. They clip rows of pencils and ballpoint pens into the pockets of their Western-style shirts and carry calculators in their cars. Were it not for the working cowboy boots under their boot-cut workpants, such managers and supervisors might well look at home in a meeting of NASA engineers.

In the Dry Creek Valley, we try to live up to that ideal, but ours are typically much smaller operations where one man tries to do it all: managing, supervising and working in the field. During the winter, we tend to look like out-of-work tractor drivers with fingers scoured, jeans cleaned and patched and Big Mac workshirts ironed. In spring, we look as though we had found work, and only the hair under our hat is ungrimed by the end of each day. From summer through harvest, we often look as though we had been transferred to the maintenance yard. The eclectic stains in our shirts have no more time to work out than does the black grease ingrained in our palms, and only the most gifted can avoid mechanic's knuckle, the raw, red scars made each time a wrench slips.

Respectfully cleaned, I once spent several days at a technical seminar with a San Joaquin Valley farm manager, who ran 4,000 acres of vineyard in 12,000 acres of mixed farming operations on the west side of the southern San Joaquin Valley. He knew his several cropping businesses inside out; knew, from memory, how many field mice an automatic tomato harvester could accidentally suck up in one eight-hour shift without having the health inspector order it shut down and how many miles of seeded, fertilized vegetable beds another machine could mound without readjustment.

I learned a great deal by listening in those days, but the memory that has hung on most vividly is the manager's description of a vineyard near Bakersfield with planted rows that were four miles long. During spring cultivation, his tractor drivers turned their roaring rigs only twice in each eight-hour shift.

Now ours is a crumpled country, without the sense of vastness that sits on the flat, fertile floor of the valley made by the San Joaquin River. There one can stand on the only kind of prominence around, the embankment of an irrigation canal, and watch vineyard rows come together in the haze at the horizon. Locally, we call that other valley the "Big Valley," perhaps because our own has such uncompromising horizons stacked so close on every hand. To the west, literally at the end of some vineyard rows in the Dry Creek Valley, four folds of the California Coastal Range rise so suddenly and so sharply that at a certain point in each summer sunset the four ridges stand, apparently, as closely together as mountains cut from paper and pasted into a diorama. The ridges are so sharp, in those mountains that

protect us from the cold ocean, and the valleys are so narrow that fire-fighting bulldozers must let themselves down along the hillsides, rolling on their tilted treads but also hanging by the steel cables spooling off their rear-mounted winches, like so many yellow mechanical spiders.

The western horizon, made of seacoast stood on end and covered with redwood and fir, curves to the north and closes the valley there, where the Coastal Range joins the Mendocino highlands. Dry Creek is born up there, about thirty-five river miles away from its mouth on the Russian River, but only in its last thirteen miles has the creek fanned and meandered enough to spread and settle arable soil. These last thirteen miles before the creek drops into the Russian River make up the Dry Creek Valley known to wine drinkers.

Those long, level rows in the vineyard near Bakersfield would have reached halfway up the spine of the entire planted area of the Dry Creek Valley. They were longer than our valley is wide at its widest point. When we pull implements through the moist spring soil, our tractors must turn and turn and turn again to avoid roads, creek banks, bluffs and swales. There are wet spots all over the landscape where springs or accumulated runoff turn the ground into sticky tractor traps. In twelve minutes of driving down a long vineyard row here, a farmer can turn up from two to as many as five different soil types. Seen from the air, the Dry Creek Valley seems to lie like an unsmoothed quilt with a jumbled patchwork of different kinds and colors of soils on its floor and hummocks and folds, creeks and creases, lifting and blocking the surface all over.

It is not the soils that make Dry Creek suitable country for excellent wines in a modern farming era, nor is it our size. The key, according to winemakers, who can taste the difference, is the valley climate. The Dry Creek Valley climate is an intense replica of that in the nearby Napa Valley, but it is framed in a smaller area, with less cachet and thus slightly less expensive grapes. Until estate-bottling wineries grew up in each of these places over the wine boom years, most of the grapes grown in the Dry Creek Valley, the

The western wall of the narrow Dry Creek Valley is the Pacific Coastal Range. Beyond it lies the ocean.

larger Alexander Valley next door to the east and the Russian River Valley around the bend to the south went farther south still in tanker trucks and later turned up as the quality and the taste in good jug wines sold nationwide. Even today, it would be hard to count the number of good, dry house reds and whites in restaurants across the United States that got their character and their breeding here. In recent years, there has been a lot of the special recognition that comes with gold medals from the competitive tastings held at the county fairs in Los Angeles and Orange County for the wines grown in our climate, then made and bottled here.

Each fogless summer day here is hot, often holding well above 80 degrees until seven in the evening. Within an hour of sunset, however, the temperature will have dropped to near 60 degrees, and it will touch 50 before morning. Cool air from the Pacific, blowing through the ridges and forested valleys from the northwest or flowing inland up the Russian River Valley from the south, holds the sugar the sun has pumped into the grapes all day, and in the cool of the night lets each wine grape blend the sugar with fruit acids. Fruit sugar makes the alcohol at the heart of any wine, and any hot climate in the temperate zone will do for sugar; but it is the acids with unfamiliar names—tannic, malic and lactic—that give wines their taste and texture.

Summer heat, the day and night heat that makes Big Valley summers infamous, keeps grape sugars high there in much heavier crops than we can raise north of San Francisco, but that hot, stable, high-pressure air also cooks off the acids. Think of the Big Valley as an ocean of air, slow to heat or cool off; then think of our little valley as a pool in a stream, heated by the sun each day and cooled by the current every night. By reason of the daily curve of temperatures, acids stay in our grapes, and that is why the Dry Creek Valley is becoming known as the best place in California to grow and make Zinfandel. All our local wines are clear in taste and strong in texture, but the best Zinfandels made here occasionally have so much of both that wine writers, quick with an adjective, tend to call them "chewy" or even "brambly."

Like our neighbors just to the southeast in the Napa Valley, we have microclimates: little areas, for example, where the cool sea air eddies and pools and the grapes for dry white wines such as Pinot Chardonnay and Sauvignon Blanc do well, or favored heights where the fog burns off first and the afternoon sun clings longest, where red-wine grapes, such as the Zinfandels, the Cabernets Sauvignon and others are happiest. Our microclimates seem smaller and more clearly defined here than those in Napa; indeed, everything about our growing conditions seems more intense and more closely compressed than those in the Napa Valley.

We get more rainfall by half again, at least. Our summers are as long and as dry, but the hot spells peak more quickly and cool off faster. The sharper contrasts here now make, and apparently have made through one century of farming, for riskier agriculture than that which has been practiced over the years in the Napa Valley. There is architectural evidence of Napa's more settled and successful character on the farming floor of that valley, where large redwood Victorian houses, the mark of the rich in nineteenth-century California, stand proudly in the middle of many vineyards. There are only four of those on the Dry Creek Valley floor, and only two of those four are kept in good repair by farm income.

The northernmost adobe on the northernmost royal land grant in Spanish California still survives here, and its small, rough outlines are not much less grand than most of what has been built since. Our nineteenth-century buildings are, typically, four-room California farmhouses, at most about thirty feet on a side, with rough-milled redwood planks, a fat twelve inches wide and one inch thick, nailed edge to edge for walls inside and smooth-milled redwood planks lapped outside for sheathing. They were built without insulation and have only their tall, empty attics for summer cooling and, originally, only cordwood and stoicism for winter heating. Until recently, when nonfarming residents began to build homes here, all houses were painted white with scant dark trim. There is still a tang of the

Above: The summer sun builds sugar content in grapes, which determines the strength of the wines they will make.

Left: The fog from the Pacific, or the night breeze from the ocean, cools the coastal valleys north of San Francisco every evening in Napa, Sonoma and Mendocino counties, sealing the subtlest flavors into the wine grapes grown there.

Richard Mounts, a Dry Creek Valley farmer.

frontier in the Dry Creek Valley, and there are those about who call the forty-five-minute drive over low mountains to the settled Napa Valley "going back east."

On a geologist's map of California, the low mountains of the Mayacamas Range, which separate the Dry Creek and Alexander valleys from the Napa Valley, show up like a seamed palm. They are full of named and unnamed earthquake faults. Nonetheless, that range rising all along our eastern horizon looks quite ordinary from the valley floor, except where Mt. St. Helena closes our horizons in the southeast. That sleeping volcano, which gave the Napa Valley its collection of volcanic soils, dominates the full circular sweep of all our horizons. It is not a lofty mountain, but it draws every eye.

So far as Mt. St. Helena is concerned, we have the advantage over the whole Napa Valley. From our distance and our westerly angle, we can see that mountain at the head of their valley clearly, make out the perfectly sloping sides of the dead cone and follow, too, the mountain's moods. Mt. St. Helena has a different face for every scrap of weather and a color for every angle of the sun.

The low, black clouds that trail behind each winter storm catch on Mt. St. Helena's shoulders like a cape and billow there as the storm clears and the grey mountain stares westward. At least once each winter, after a cold storm from the Gulf of Alaska has closed around the mountain, the clouds unfurl and stream eastward, leaving a light, white mantling of snow that rarely lasts through a full day's sunshine.

The mountain is impenetrable onyx black on those spring mornings when we are sweating out the possibility of a predawn frost and we look to the south and east for relief. The sun rises there, over Mt. St. Helena's left shoulder, and with it comes safety. On those mornings, we can see and judge every subtle shading from dark to light, because each one marks a minute closer to warmth. The sky behind the mountain changes first from pale grey to amethyst pink while a still lighter shade of pink seeps down its upper slopes. Minutes later, in the cold red light of dawn, that pink

Mt. St. Helena, the dead volcano that closes off the northern end of the Napa Valley and rises beyond the mouth of the Dry Creek Valley, dominates almost every view.

Two generations of Teldeschis: Gary, left, and Ray, with their father, Mike, in the family vineyard.

on the mountain deepens and is molded by the first shadows of the day. Immediately to the north, plumes of steam from venting geysers stand like shapeless black sentinels on the eastern ridge, then fade to cloud color with the saving sun.

Mt. St. Helena does not soar over hundreds of square miles, the way other West Coast volcanic peaks such as Shasta, Hood and Rainier seem to do. It is an older, milder mountain than those and has acquired barely noticeable tricks to stay at the visual focus of the local horizon. The mountain does not rise from among the cornstalks as do some Mexican volcanoes, yet it appears to stand at the end of each easterly vineyard row on every working morning. It heaves clear of the spring and summer farming dust, full of brown folds and dark green shadows, even under the heavy midday light that flattens every other contour and washes out nearer colors. Mt. St. Helena catches and molds the salmon pink light from the sun setting in the Pacific each summer evening and turns it into mauve on the ridges and purple in the swales.

The mountain is our magic monolith, our moonstone. The harvest moon, October's full, which signals the end of the growing season, seems to leap from the throat of Mt. St. Helena's cold cone and hang just above it for minutes on end, golden and bloated, before it turns slowly silver and becomes again the moving moon.

There may be something about Mt. St. Helena, about all our low mountains, something about the small scale of our vineyard country that stirs a comforting ancestral memory of the Appennines and Lucca. Certainly all those descended from emigrants from that winemaking corner of Italy who now live here are happily at home. Among the established farming families in the Dry Creek Valley there are, in alphabetical order: Amanns, Auradous, several Blacks, the Krecks, the Mounts and the Nelsons, all descended from northern Europeans. There are three families of Petersens, who have been here for three generations, and the Phillips, whose ancestors held the Spanish land grant called the Rancho Tzabaco and who have married the Schmidts. There are the Rueds, father and son. However, there are four families of Teldeschis, transplanted from Lucca, farming in the valley and two—no, three now—of Rafanellis. There are three Buchignani families from that region actively farming, and there have been more. There are the Cuneos, who count themselves as Genoese, the Sainis and two Guadagnis still farming full time.

I cannot recall whether it was Jim or Fred Guadagni, or one of Fred's two sons, who once put an end to a conversation that was turning plaintive in tone, about the changes that have come into the valley with nonfarming neighbors, with a huge new federal dam across the creek and lower grape prices. The Guadagnis' shop, where Fred's sons, Joe and Don, weld and fabricate farming machinery for the rest of us, is a pleasant place for farmers to gather and complain. That day, though, the speculation about an uncertain future stopped at the certainty from one man who had found his place.

"Where else would a man want to go anyway?" the second- or third-generation Guadagni of Dry Creek asked. "There's no place better."

That said, there was nothing further for those dawdling around the space heater in the Guadagnis' shop to do but to get back to work.

Americo Rafanelli and his son David in the family winery.

CHAPTER FOUR

Willows and Swallows

Willow buds, blowing like dusty green pennants on the advancing edge of spring, signal the end of winter and the year's first deep turn. The long, gauzy buds dancing from every branch of the willows along Dry Creek are the first serious warning to a grape grower that dormancy is over. Three to four weeks later, the first swallow to catch the corner of his eye marks the end of the slippery, risky slide into spring and the beginning of the hard business of the growing year. Both harbingers mean that the rush that follows budbreak and runs with the first flush of growth from the vines is about to burst upon every grower.

Sometime between willows and swallows a man needs to be as ready as he can be. Sometime between willows and swallows it all seems to start at once: frost protection, tillage, spraying, cultivation and worrying. Before the willows even show green, however, like the tide starting to run at the beaches before it moves the deeper waters of a bay, the urgency of the growing season to come reaches up into the end of winter and stirs everything and everyone about a vineyard. It is a trying, anxious time in late January or early February when the days are growing longer and the need for action begins to press on vines and people, but when there is still no ready action crying out to be done. It takes people in different ways. I have known my nearest neighbor, in this transition time, to paint his truck, build and install a new monogrammed headboard for it, put new brakes and final drives into his Caterpillar, button it up and paint it, then start rebuilding his fork lift before the need to start turning dirt struck clear and hard. When I was brand-new at the vineyard business, I once found myself, in this time, going at the normally pleasant annual chore of making willow cuttings and sticking them into the creek bank to root, as though it were a time trial. And I could not tell why.

Juan and Miguel Silva.

Physiologically, the vines have begun to respond to the slowly lengthening days and hesitantly warming soil, and sap has started to push up through their dry and dormant trunks. Farmers call it "moving" and say, for example, that pears, which come first here, or prunes, or, finally, grapes are moving. The unmistakable sign that they are moving is a slight, white, puffy swelling at the edge of the scales around each bud. Pruning cuts may also bleed a bit of clear white fluid in the warmest part of the day. It is possible that the farming urge starts to move in the people who work year-round in vineyards at the same time.

Wine from the previous year's harvest, sleeping in barrels, stirs as if it remembered the rush of blood in the vines that bore it. Chemists call the stirring "secondary fermentation" and explain that it is due to residual sugar and also to bacteria acting on the wine's malic acid and converting it to weaker lactic acid. But, even in climate-controlled wine cellars, the stirring unmistakably happens at the same time the sap begins to rise in the vineyards outside.

Americo Rafanelli, the sturdy and hardily cheerful winemaker who farms the vineyard next south from me, knows all the names and explanations for the process, and well he ought, since he has been making wine here well into his sixties, as his father did before him. It was Rafanelli who explained the technicalities of malo-lactic fermentation to me. However, when he first mentioned it, on a February day we met by chance at the property line and began to wonder out loud when the growing season might begin, he said, "The wine moves, too, you know. It will sleep all winter and then, just when the vines move, if you've got any sugar left in it, the wine will stir and start fermenting again. You can't touch it until June."

That last phrase could stand well as a description of a grower's disposition, which becomes very touchy in the spring of every year when the winter's contemplation is coming to an end as the willows bloom, when everything around him starts to stir, quicken and change. The exigencies of a natural process take over his life, beginning at this point, and it is almost as though a grower felt the change begin as his vines do. Running hard through the ensuing four months to keep up with the growing vines can often be irritating and is never entirely easy. At the grimy end of winter in a vineyard, we all seem to feel the hard time coming.

In the pruning season of 1980, Miguel Silva, my best hired hand and leading pruner, bought his first car at the uneasy time just before spring and probably hastened the changes at work in himself. Miguel is a large young man, with a broad forehead and face made square by a wide smile with many even teeth. In the spring of 1979, he had come looking for work on a polished ten-speed bicycle. His relatives working with me then, an uncle and a cousin quite removed, called him "Caterpillar," and the physical frame for his nickname was clear.

Miguel was eighteen when he first came to work, but his shoulders spread well beyond the handlebars of his bicycle and he looked quite too big for its delicate frame. Moving through a pattern well known to all California farmers, the uncle saw to it that Miguel got on with the *patron*, then took his courtly leave and returned to their village in the mountains of Guanajuato, north of Mexico City. The cousin survived a labor crisis at our place that nonetheless scarred his pride, and by late summer he had drifted off to a town job in a sawmill. But, just then, Miguel's thin and witty younger brother, Juan, arrived and my complement of two hired hands was complete again. The extended Mexican family, in a seamless and apparently rational way, had simultaneously taken care of their own and of me. Jobs at my place were still in their family, there was work for the newcomers and I had never been without help at a busy time. The pattern had protected us all.

Border Patrol raids were more frequent that summer than is normal to the north of San Francisco, and even those whose papers are in order do not like dealing with the aspiring Texas Ranger types who seem to work for the Patrol, searching agricultural counties for illegal aliens. Simultaneously, a chain of circumstances, which later ended with the discrimination case in court, closed around the old town plaza, which had been a fairly comfortable place to loiter each Sunday. The Guadalajara and La Potranca, two bars on the plaza where Spanish only had been spoken, lost their leases and closed.

After that, many of Miguel's extended family, their friends and their friends' friends brought their weekend beer out to our farm instead of the plaza. Saturday and Sunday afternoons grew very loud at the two-bedroom house where Miguel and Juan lived, alongside the county road between our hill vineyard and the pear orchard. The brothers, however, did not drink. With hospitable smiles, they cleaned up each weekend after uncles and in-laws, cousins and godparents. They went off to the store for tortillas and milk, cigarettes and huge cans of jalapeño peppers. From one departing relative, they inherited a Chrysler from another era, with tall tailfins and crumpled fenders. It had one green door and a brown body mottled with patches of red primer paint. The car was named El Rey, and for a few weeks that summer the brothers treated it like a king. They cleaned it inside and out. They stood near it every afternoon after work and watched over it on weekends. Then, in early August, they bought a battery and prevailed on the sawmill cousin to drive El Rey for them every weekend.

Through the rest of the summer, with the earnestness that characterized his work in the field, Miguel learned to drive the Chrysler. He studied the California driver's manual in Spanish and passed his licensing test. The King was his, and Juan rode the ten-speed bicycle on all the errands that fall to a younger brother. However, every weekend Juan and the sawmill cousin rode out in the Chrysler. Miguel drove.

During the harvest of his first year, Miguel unfolded the friendly big man's unassertive kind of leadership. He gathered a crew of friends around him and made a practice of asking how everyone else was doing during each day's picking, so that he could keep track and make sure that his crew of youths outpicked the men in other crews every day. He made money, but he did not join in the daily harvest routine, for most other men, of a six-pack at the end of every working day.

"You know, it makes me feel seasick if I drink beer the way the others do," Miguel told me after that harvest. "I send my beer money home."

He kept enough, however, to replace El Rey when it suffered winter transmission troubles that were beyond us all. The Chrysler sat to one side, and, in January of 1980, right at the restless time, Miguel brought home a sober blue Oldsmobile coupe. Almost simultaneously, his earnestness at work slowly began to fade. It seemed difficult on some pruning days to get an early start. Mondays were particularly hard, and I noticed that Juan, for the first time, was left behind on weekends. The two began to snap at each other at work.

"He has other friends now," Juan said, when I asked him about this. "He's doing other things."

The younger brother pedaled Miguel's bicycle along the wet winter roads alone. One white morning of frost late in January, he came to work alone.

"Where's Miguel?" I asked.

"He didn't come," Juan said.

"He didn't come home, or he didn't come to work?"

"No."

"No, what?"

"No, he did come home, but he can't come to work."

"Well," I asked, "is he still drunk?" Such a reflection on his brother was too much for Juan.

"No, he's not drunk, now," he said quickly. "He smashed his car and he smashed his face and he can hardly move. He can't work. Today."

We walked back to the help house together and found Miguel rolled up in two blankets on the faded red velour couch against a wall of their living room. On one wall calendar hanging above his head, the Blessed Virgin held her hand to her heart. On the adjoining wall, facing away, a blonde calendar girl with a butterfly tattoo at her navel hooked the fingers of one hand into her waistband and smiled. Miguel stared straight up, at the ceiling. His left eye was purple, swollen shut, and the whole cheek beneath it was covered with a bandage stained by new blood. The

The Silva brothers.

front tooth that had anchored the left half of his dazzling smile was gone.

So, apparently, was his trust. He pushed past my questions about his injuries and medical care, almost as though these were matters of no concern. What seemed important was to make me believe his account of the accident.

" I had slowed down to try to turn around," he said, "because we didn't know the road. And when I pulled over to stop, you know, the road had no shoulder, just a ditch. And we went into it and we couldn't get the car out.

"So some friends took us to the hospital," he went on. "I was slowed way down. I just didn't know the road."

The blue Olds never returned and we never talked of it again.

"I lost my tooth," Miguel told me that morning, without smiling. "I lost my tooth, but tomorrow we'll be back at work. We've got to finish pruning."

The truth was that Miguel was tired of pruning, tired of the sloppy ground and the rain, the bare vines and the morning frosts. Like all of us at that time of the year, he wanted an end to it. The dying winter tastes about as fresh as a day-old bandage at that time of year. It clogs the ears and makes everyone impatient for the change that each can feel is about to happen. That anxiety can make a man do things he otherwise might not have tried. It happened that Miguel's anxiety coincided with his American coming of age. He drank beer, he drove and he totaled his car and walked away alive.

We stopped pruning for three days while I arranged the dental work that eventually repaired Miguel's smile. He seemed more thankful for the time off. Without any apparent smugness, he insisted on paying the dentist himself. Two weeks after work resumed, he bought a green Plymouth Fury, which we called El Principe, the Prince, and its reign lasted for two years.

"It belonged to an old *gringa* who only drove it around town," Miguel assured me solemnly. "And to church on Sundays."

Chopping up the vineyard
prunings.

One of the secrets of any acculturation process must lie in learning to accept the myths of the new culture uncritically.

During the car crisis, the year had turned. The stark winter outline of the bare trees along the creek bank had softened as the willow buds opened, lengthened and fuzzed. After three weeks without significant rain, Dry Creek had dropped back into a settled channel between its gravel bars, and the water had cleared from winter brown to the cold, milky blue-green of spring flows. With each day, an extra few minutes of daylight from a sun each day slightly higher in the southern sky had begun to dry out the soil and make the whole vineyard a more cheerful-looking place, because the long, mean shadows cast by winter's low sun had begun shrinking toward spring positions and swelling, putting on soft bulk.

We were heading through the last winter jobs, pruning proceeding apace, and could feel winter coming to an end. By the end of the first week in February, there was even a foretaste of spring warmth by way of promise that the anxiety would pass, that there would be time and weather to finish winter work and to be ready for the day in March when the loose lumps lying on top of the ground between vine rows would dry to just the right point—dry on top and damp below, crumbling easily in the hand—to jump on the tractor and start working ground.

"Friday, February 8. Clear. Warm. Springlike weather," my field log entry for that day reads.

"Saturday, February 9. Clear. 28° frost. Prune Carignane. Chop all Zins. Paid," the log continues, and it was beautiful work on a beautiful day. The use of the word "all" means that I was able to drive through all three of the wet spots in that ten-acre block of Zinfandel, dragging the howling brush chopper through places that normally might have swallowed tractor and chopper into mud up to the hubs.

That was the last winter a little red-tail hawk nested in an oak on the hill above the Zinfandel, and he hunted with me that day. Driving a tractor over the prunings lying like thin, jumbled skeletons in the vineyard rows and flailing them into chunks that later will be turned into the soil also levels the grass and mows down the winter weeds between vine rows. Tractor and chopper leave behind strips of uneven lawn between the rows, and anything moving is without cover.

The hawk knew this. He knew, too, that the onrushing tractor would scare the wits out of young jackrabbits or mice who had been born and raised that winter in the protective tangle of prunings and grasses. So the hawk flew, quite sparingly of any effort, from sprinkler to sprinkler about four rows away, paralleling my advance and probably keeping that distance out of fear of me. I imagine that the brush chopper, noisy as it is, struck him as nothing more than a yellow hive full of very large, very angry bees screaming at one another and bouncing off the inside walls of their moving steel hive in a rage.

When a rabbit started, then froze in fear, the red-tail had only to pump his wings twice for enough altitude to sight his prey. He stooped quite elegantly, almost fastidiously, his grey wings gripping at the air and his rusty red underbody showing only at the moment when he flared them and struck. Twice that Saturday I stamped on the clutch and stopped, engine roaring and chopper screaming, while the hawk made his quick, neat kills.

There was time to watch the hawk that day, time to appreciate our odd symbiosis, and still time to finish the whole block and do a week's payroll for the three men pruning with Miguel. There was time the next day to drop the chopper from the tractor and rerig the tractor with the sprayer, and to set the sprayer and booms for herbicide application.

Time in hand, and a flexible appreciation for it, is the simple secret of survival farming, which works out to be just keeping up with the work. Successful farming, of course, requires much more, including temperament, intuition, technical competence, business acumen and a fair measure of good fortune. But a sense for time and the rhythms of nature, much like the sense a boatman working his way through surf must have, resting and preparing in the lulls, watching the waves and being in place, ready to pull when the right wave lifts: this sense will probably keep a grower going in the temporary or permanent absence of other gifts. Such a sense enables a man to keep up without exhaustion. No matter what the crop, certain things *must* be done at a certain time, accomplished during a certain single stage in the crop's yearly life, put in place before a certain danger appears. In our game, some farmers I have known are fond of saying, God makes the rules. There is no appeal, no sense of fair or unfair. The process just happens and a grower must be ready for it.

As dormancy thinned and lifted in 1980, I was ready. On Monday, February 11, I sprayed herbicides on the weeds and grasses left in the thirty-six-inch-wide strip running from foot to foot of each vine in their rows. There, where the chopper and disc harrow do not reach, it works out to be less expensive to control weeds around the vines by spraying each row with a mix of herbicides during winter dormancy than it would be to let them grow and put a crew of men to work hoeing them away the following spring.

Chopping up the brush and spraying for year-long weed control both require running tractors over wet ground, and that implies the worst in soil compaction, which is hard on vine roots over the long term. Most often, however, it is the short term that looms largest for a grower with a mortgage. To pay off his mortgage, he must produce as much as possible as cheaply as possible each and every year for a lifetime. He finds himself looking hard at the short term, out of economic necessity, and gritting his teeth over the longer term.

There, caught in the short term on February 11, I made a nervous note to myself in the field log: "Colombard fuzzing?" The week's notes continued:

Tuesday, February 12. Lincoln's Birthday. Fog. 35°. Prune Carignane. Strip spray Zins. Hi ground dried out.

Wednesday, February 13. Clear. 31° frost. Prune Carignane. Strip spray finish Zins; two loads on Carign.

Thursday, February 14. Rain. Trace. Warm. Finish prune Carignane.

Finally, a reassuring note to myself: "No sign bud movement." The week had ended well, with only one block of nine acres left to prune, meaning six to eight days' work and three weeks, perhaps even a month, to do it in, if budbreak came near mid-March as it usually does. There was time in hand.

The men could finish pruning the Colombard, left until the last on purpose, while I rerigged tractor and implements, moved the main pump and all its connecting pipes from winter storage and put the pump back on its landing on the creek bank. I would be working at the foot of the vineyard block where the crew would be pruning, and could be available while I flushed out the filter above the pump, maneuvered the pump itself into position, set up and tested all its connections. The men could break off pruning to help me at the stages requiring manhandling or someone on the bank while I was in the water. We seemed well positioned to meet the first big deadline of the growing season: to have the pump and thirty-five acres of overhead sprinklers ready for frost protection before the buds broke open and pushed out new, green growth.

There was no reason to fret when the rain thickened on Friday, the fifteenth. The field log entries for that day and the next few, with rainfall recorded at seven in the morning for the preceding twenty-four hours, as is my habit, were matter-of-fact:

Friday, February 15. Rain 0.40″. No help.

Saturday, February 16. Rain 3.75″. No help.

Sunday, February 17. Rain 0.50″. No help.

Monday, February 18. Rain 5.00″. No help.

Five inches of rain in twenty-four hours is not unusual on the west side of Dry Creek Valley, where twenty years of figures kept by one neighbor show an average annual rainfall approaching sixty inches. The creek was bank full during the day, then receded as the rain slackened in the afternoon. Overnight, another storm climbed on top of the remnants of the five-inch storm. The field log for the next day:

Vineyard pruned and ready for
chopping.

Tuesday, February 14. Rain 2.30″. No help. DRY CREEK WASHED OUT MAIN PUMP SITE.

It is hard to describe the feeling that came crawling up from under me, numbing feet, knees, hips and intestines as it rose to the diaphragm, when I first saw what the flooding creek had done. Might it be like the shock that first follows a bad stomach wound? I stopped and looked away. Then I started walking again, pacing off distance and trying to put together a remedy in my mind.

The creek was still running at the top of its banks, the water a thin brown color in the light from the south just after sunrise. The current, a hundred feet wide or more, raced toward that low light, and hard little waves stood for an instant, then fell, where it roiled and writhed and turned on itself. Logs, trees and smaller debris floated past at the pace of a fast trotting horse. There was no wind left, so the loudest noises came from the water rushing past the bank. It piled up against the crumbling soil at the edge of the vineyard, eddied away and came back again with a heavy, sucking sound.

Where the bank had been, knotted down by the roots of mature willows and underbrush so thick the quail had been forced to walk through it, there was only the noisy, brown current. For 150 feet, beginning above the pump landing, a 45-degree slope of soil, fifteen to twenty feet wide and thick with trees, had gone in the night, trees and all.

Of course it was not as bad as a stomach wound; not even as bad as having the edges of that same flood lick into your home and stand soaking, distorting and soiling forever everything that was yours in that safe place. However, for a stark instant, I saw myself unable to put the pump in at the point where all its thousands of yards of piping came out on the bank, saw my vineyard without any protection, saw the buds swell, stretch and burst, saw them unfold one, then two, pairs of leaves and the first embryonic grape clusters, and saw the first spring freeze rise from the bare, white ground and leave one year's crop withered, black and drooping, dead before it had grown.

It had happened to my predecessor on this farm one year, before he had installed sprinklers, and I had asked his son what that farmer had done.

"He bought two hundred-pound sacks of dry beans and that's what my parents ate all year," he answered.

There is a farming expression to explain a sudden clout of misfortune: "It's always something." I remembered the phrase that morning as I measured, and also the corollary that there is alway something a man can do. The high, whiny hum of panic receded in my head.

Placing grape brush to protect the pump site.

CHAPTER FIVE

Getting Through It

Frost is a clear, capricious killer. Our spring freezes rise from the ground, congealing as they climb the vines. On some frost mornings the freezing level stays below a man's knee, stiffening the grass and turning it white. On others, the bad ones, the frost rises to bud level on the vines before midnight and can coat them with ice before dawn. It takes only one half hour at 31 degrees Fahrenheit to kill new growth by freezing the water inside each cell in the translucent green tips. Freezing water expands and shatters the tenuous cell walls. The danger is gone soon after sunrise, but by midafternoon following a frost in an unprotec-ted vineyard, the new green shoots will blacken, collapse and hang like mourner's ribbons on the vines. The technical name for such freezing is radi-ation frost, and the meteorologists' explanation is that on clear, still nights with a cold, transparent air mass above soil that is not yet fully warm, the ground radiates its accumu-lated heat and loses it to the black spaces high in the earth's atmosphere. A farmer can feel that happening on his uncov-ered head in the clear, still dark while he waits out in the vineyard, watching the temperature at bud height. Without a hood or hat, body heat leaves his head, and his scalp be-gins to tingle as though indi-vidual hairs were stirring in the invisible thermal current.

Radiation sets another cooling process in motion when the soil in hill vineyards cools. The heavier, cold air at ground level slips, so to speak, and be-gins to slither downhill, where it flows like an unseen current in the night, filling in the flats and pooling against tree lines or fences. The process is called a cold air drain, and I have heard farmers on the mid-Atlantic coast call it a cold air draw, or a water draw, and bless it be-cause the cool air draining down a draw or a waterway in the night will cool off any house standing along its way on the sweltering summer nights peculiar to that region.

Frost protection with sprinklers at dawn.

Above: Mild frost damage to grape leaves and embryonic clusters in their first week of growth.

Right: A frost sunset flares behind a sprinkler head.

In the northern California wine country in the spring, a cold air drain is no blessing. It concentrates the effects of a freeze in one vineyard and may siphon it away from others. More than half of my planted acreage lies at the mouth of a three-mile-long canyon, and the drain is so strong I can feel it if I stand with my back to the hills. The cold air flows past, almost but not quite whispering as it bites the edges of my ears. The canyon's cold air drain pools on my fifty flat acres, making them about one degree colder on any given morning than the forty acres just to the south along the hills, and several degrees colder than the vineyard to the north. When it freezes, on my acreage, I may be out for three hours before dawn with my pumps, while my neighbor to the north pulls the blankets around his ears and need not get up until the sun does.

Frost is not a threat on every night; in fact, it comes only rarely in the dangerous period between budbreak and mid-May, by which time the soil below the vines will have captured enough heat to keep the air above it warm on clear nights. There is a National Weather Service forecaster in residence for that period, making and issuing forecasts twice daily for the wine-growing regions of Napa and Sonoma counties. And a farmer can almost always tell when he's going to get a freeze: the heat goes out of the spring sun by 3:30 on the afternoon before, and if the wind dies at sunset and the night sky is absolutely cloudless, he's in for it. The sun sets on those nights with a chilly red glow that shades quickly up the sky to grey, to blue and then to black, as if some huge, steel-rolling mill were sending back its light, without any heat, from an immense distance beyond the western hills.

The threat of a freeze beetles over a farmer's joy in the blank miracle of new growth bursting from his dormant vines. That threat can drag at him like a tethered weight after he smiles once at the vines, then puts his head down and drives to get through it. "Getting through it" is the local phrase that covers all the work that must be done before the vine rows grow closed in May or June, and a three-hour vigil

in 34-degree dark, waiting for the the thermometer to dip toward 32 degrees, will tell sometime during the following day when a man tries to put in ten hours on a tractor.

Something gives. I have found myself nodding off to sleep, after lunch, in the tractor seat. And another farmer, recalling the spring of 1976, when there were twelve straight nights of killer frosts, said, "You can get so you hear the frost alarm, roll over and say the hell with it. Let 'em freeze."

Realistically, that option simply is not open to a farmer with a mortgage. For such a man, there are three economically comfortable ways available to protect vines from the killing clutch of a freeze. He can plant on hills, from whence the cold air drains away to be constantly replaced by warmer air. There are wind machines, tall steel tubes with airplane engines mounted on them thirty feet off the ground. Wind machines, which make the Napa Valley resound in a cold dawn like an old carrier flight deck, were developed to pull down the heated air that hangs just above the San Joaquin Valley floor every night in a thermocline and to blow it around the endangered crop below like a moving blanket. In the narrow coastal valleys, however, there is no thermocline; so wind machines must be used with a protective fence of return stack heaters—dangerous, diesel-fueled devices that look like upended tin amphorae and heat a curtain of hot air for the wind machines to shove around.

Water, applied by overhead sprinklers at a steady rate of twelve-hundredths of an inch per hour is by far the best available means of keeping grapevines alive. Such a steady, artificial rain staves off frost damage in three ways: it raises the dew point and thereby holds up the temperature at which vapor in the air will form hoar frost; it acts imperfectly, as fog or a cloud overhead would, slowing down the radiation loss of heat; and, finally, when the temperature drops below 30 degrees, the water spread by the sprinklers encases the vines in ice. So long as the ice keeps forming at regular intervals every few seconds, the heat released when water turns to ice is absorbed by the green tissues inside each clear, crystal case. The tissue stays at 32 degrees, out of danger. So runs the theory. In practice, it is a very eerie thing for a farmer to see ice building around the green buds on which his future rides. If his pump stops, for any of the accidental reasons that haunt running machines, before that ice melts, the buds freeze and the crop they might have formed is lost. Depending on when in the spring a killer freeze comes, there might be some regrowth, but such regrowth does not replace the loss entirely.

After Dry Creek tore away the land where my main pump stood on February 19, 1980, my highest, most pressing priority was to carve out a flat ledge, protected from the creek, where the pump could stand until May and make rain on demand. The bank left behind by the dropping flood was a sheer face of crumbling, sandy soil about eighteen feet high from gravel bar to crest. Any two- or three-inch storm could swell the creek enough to melt the bank away, as it had, in fact, melted away acres from vineyards planted on the banks downstream in the previous ten years.

The accumulated years of local experience in trying to keep Dry Creek from taking back the soil it has given have distilled out three proven methods. The most elegant—and most expensive—is to painstakingly place heavy quarried rock along the threatened bank. A quicker, cheaper variant is to shove chunks of broken pavement over the edge to form a haphazard rock facing known as rip-rap. The quickest and classically cheapest way of holding a bank is to tumble stripped car bodies into the current to form a steel wall between it and the exposed soil. All three have practical approval from the California Department of Fish and Game, but in Sonoma County a neighbor who does not like the sight of a grower's car bodies may be able to move the county to order him to abate his eyesore.

I waited until the end of February, but the weather stayed too wet to bring in the heavy trucks that move rip-rap. On the twenty-eighth, two white-grape vines that grow on warm and favored ground at the edge of the barnyard and therefore begin every step in the growing process as much as a week before the production vines, opened their buds scales and began showing the puffy brown gauze through which the growing points break. I found three totally stripped car bodies. The junkyard hauled them to the edge of the vineyard at the paved road. Quickly and self-consciously, I snaked them through the mud a quarter of a mile to the pump site, cabled them together, bound them to deadmen on the bank and shoved them in. Still hurrying the following week, I gathered piles of pruning brush as tall as a man, rolled them over the edge and wired them in place to completely cover the car bodies and to collect silt from the current, a process that can, over years, recover a new bank from the creek.

However, I was not quick enough to escape the irony of the farmer who works the vineyard directly across the creek, an old-line Italian. "I see where my environmentalist neighbor across the creek has discovered car bodies," he told a salesman, who told me. "These new guys all learn in time."

The willows were in full leaf. The first swallow returned on March 10, the day after the main pump settled onto its new landing on the bank. The swallow dipped and tumbled alone through the wind above the creek, soaring and turning on swift, upswept wings, much as if he had been a schoolboy racing at random across his favorite playground, his arms raised in joy after weeks of being shut in by rain. The French Colombard vines in the block that begins by Dry Creek moved, pushed that week and, by the fifteenth, most precisely on the normal schedule, were showing their first pairs of leaves like little, green flags set on the brown vines to signal hope and continuity in the sunlight.

The first frost requiring pumped sprinkler protection did not come until April 3, sharpening that feeling approaching embarrassment that comes from watching things happen as though one were not there; comes with the realization that all one's haste and anxiety have not affected the unfoldings of the year's natural rhythm at all.

In a stuttering spring like that one, when the natural growing clock chases the changing weather and shifts its pace every few days, a grower must reorder his own list of

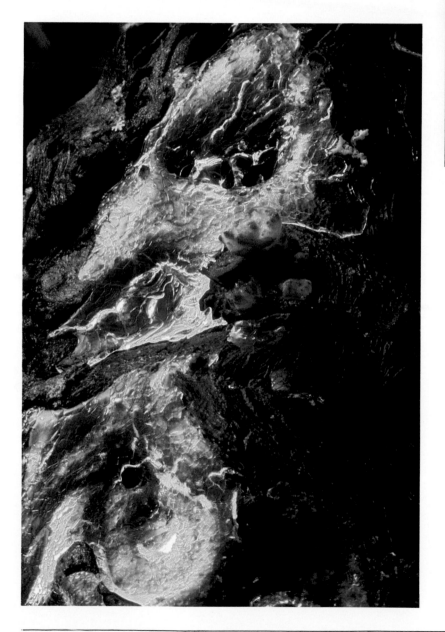

Above: The Dry Creek Valley air filled with water from protective sprinklers on a frosty morning.

Left: Ice has formed as protection against frost around vine buds.

Above: Replacing a pump
suction pipe, threatened by two
days of high water.

Right: Shoving grape prunings
over the bank to protect it from
Dry Creek at flood stage.

priorities every day according to what he sees on the ground and feels in the air. There is no getting it right beforehand. My approach that year, the approach of every "new guy," was like that of the general staff that is always prepared to fight the last war, and always stumbling to the defensive when the tactics of the present war crash over them. Two years earlier, the buds really had broken in mid-February. Frost protection was urgently required. Once it had been scrambled into place, the frost never came. Instead, that season's enemy was early botrytis, a fungus that grows best in warm, wet weather and feeds like a cancer on the succulent new shoots. A grey haze would appear on a shoot's green surface, a day later a brown spot, and two days later that shoot folded over onto itself or dropped off the vine, gone for the year along with all the grapes it might have grown.

The spring of 1980 was cold and inimical to botrytis; so I used my first dry weather to gather brush and heave it over the bank. Only after that was done did my fixed working focus widen enough to notice little, brown punctures in some of the puffing green buds and neat, semicircular slices gone from the reddish edges of others, which meant that cutworms were feeding nightly on my unborn crop. When the rain returned, it was too late and too wet to spray for lasting control; so we had to trickle baited worm poison by the handful over every vine in the affected area, between each rain.

It is always something.

The rain came and went through March, and between rains there was heat enough to harden the surface of the soil but not to dry it out enough for tillage. The rain came, then the heat, then the rain again, until at the end of the month we all were standing on acres and acres of what farmers everywhere call "ten-minute ground."

Ten-minute ground tills easily only ten minutes out of the year. Before that time it is too wet to crumble and will fall off the moldboard of a plow or the cupped turning blade of a disc harrow in sticky wet crescents of clay that dry out as hard and as misshapen as rejected bricks on a brickyard rubble pile. All year those unapologetic clods will haunt a farmer, pummeling his tractor and him if he drives through on business, turning his ankle if he walks through the vineyard and causing his pickers to curse him for an incompetent in the fall. After the ten minutes are up, the ground is so hard that a plow is out of the question, and a disc harrow, or disc, will clang and twitch but make no more than a series of ridges in the ground, from which the weeds and grass will spring back up, waving, after the tractor has passed. Some soils are born that ornery, with too much clay and not enough loam or sand, and other soils can be tortured by the weather in some years until they are as cantankerous as adobe clay. On those years, the dry explanation hereabouts is: "It's a great year for clods."

By early April, 1980 looked like a great year for clods. A visitor, hearing three of us complain one wet Sunday afternoon, asked in all innocence, "But why do farmers plow anyway?"

"Because it's in their blood," my host and his answered, with the kind of humor that a farmer with income from another business can manage. "It's only a ritual."

Tillage, cultivation or groundwork, as farmers call it, is best taken as deliberately as a ritual. It is a slow and painstaking chore, requiring great concentration and hours every day for weeks of springtime. It is the best, most economical way to clear the vineyard soil of weeds so that only the vines will feed and drink, unbothered, on the nutrients and water stored after winter in the soil. A farmer does it for weed control, a true necessity, and he does it as well as possible for pride in the appearance of his vineyard. Of a farmer who is a meticulous groundworker, a neighbor will say, "He vacuums his vineyard."

Groundwork is the backbone of spring work in the vineyard. It brings with it a lifting sense of anticipation and accomplishment when the disc first bites into ready ground, when the grainy smell of freshly turned earth is stronger than a tractor's diesel breath and when light brown soil unfurls steadily off the bright blades, folding weeds and grasses under to become part of the earth. Oat hay and mustard and

The first leaves of spring. Vine growth has begun.

quackgrass, Dallas grass and subclover, filaree, purslane, shepherd's-purse, dock and plantain rise up the turning curve of each blade of the harrow's front gang of discs, drop off, uprooted and partially buried, and disappear under the back gang.

On the very best, singing days of the first pass through the vineyard with a disc, the soil unrolls behind tractor and harrow flat, even and swollen with chopped weeds ready to rot and richen the ground. Blackbirds and sassy grackles hop and flutter just beyond the disc, stabbing at worms and grubs and quarreling over the choicest pieces. Behind them, the ungainly crows lurch and scramble pigeon-toed over the ground, hurrying like plump aldermen in black Sunday suits chasing little boys. As the aldermen might, the crows stop whenever a tractor driver looks back and strike their most noble poses, heads erect in profile, as if to say they would never stoop to muscling such urchins as grackles away from a curling red piece of worm.

On the second pass through, the ground is drier and often crankier. The disc skitters over hard ground, then bites in softer soil and swerves unpredictably, threatening the vines alongside. A farmer is fighting the stubborn, late-growing annuals, such as thistle, rye and burr clover, and the unconquerable perennials, such as Bermuda grass and Johnson grass. The latter are single champions among weeds. They grow from seed as well as from waxy rhizomes along their roots. It doesn't take books to tell a farmer that every time his disc chops a Bermuda grass root he is making two or four new plants and dragging them out to fresh soil to root. Chemical warfare is all that stops Bermuda grass. As a neighbor who shared his Bermuda grass battle plan with me said, "Disking only makes it mad."

Dust billows up beneath tractor and disc the second time through, blinding a tractor driver on a downwind turn through a row and streaming out behind on the upwind pass. Heading upwind, diesel exhaust pours past and soaks into the nose and hair. Most growers in the Dry Creek Valley seem to have taken to making this second pass with a

Above: The grower at dawn on a frost morning. He turned the pumps on just after midnight and watched the thermometer stay below freezing all night.

Right: Spring work begins in earnest with the first tilling pass through the vineyard on a tractor pulling a disc harrow.

cultivator, its wide-set shanks raking through the ground like curved iron fingers, or with a weed knife, which skims just below the surface of the soil like a raked guillotine blade. Both implements can dig out the hardy annual weeds, if driven with skill, and both minimize the dust.

There is no escaping the dust on the third time through for groundwork. It saturates the pores, stings the eyes and clogs nose and ears. It mingles with diesel fuel in the nostrils and under fingernails to create the constant odor of the season, an edgy mixture of dry and oily smells that stays on after every scrubbing shower and sticks with the grower as he sleeps.

The third pass is designed to lift the worked ground into a dry mulch that will seal soil moisture away from the sun and smooth the ground into a flat, stable working platform for all the foot and tractor work to come. The third pass also corrects earlier mistakes, and some growers can dispense with it. Those who do seem to follow every man's urge, for by this time, in May, all the exhilaration of the cool early days of spring is gone. A farmer's patience has been thinned by the pressure of work and frayed by the inevitable breakdowns and setbacks. Groundwork is now an endurance test.

The temptation is to charge out every morning at first light, check oil and water, grease the tractor, start up and get roaring down the rows by the time the sun is up, then hold on to the wheel or steering clutches, bouncing and swaying, thinking of nothing, through the heat of the day until the sun sets. Yielding to that temptation does not pay.

Giving slow and careful attention to grease fittings and gauges, fan belts and spindles, disc level and hydraulic response, and all the nuts, bolts and setscrews that hold every one of all the three-dimensional adjustments in place pays off. Such attention in the growing yellow light before sunrise prevents later trouble; it also slows a farmer's heartbeat, focuses his vision and sets a pattern of concentration that is the only way to avoid carrying away three vines at a swipe when the disc wanders in a row. There are many styles of tractor driving, from the dogged through the dashing to the gracefully artistic. However, the race of weeks through groundwork goes always to the tortoise and never to the hare.

I started vineyard tractor work some years ago with my toes curled like talons inside my workboots, trying to grip the steel footplate on the tractor in a total effort of concentration to will an eight-foot-wide disc harrow through the ten-foot-wide space between my vines without damage. I clenched my teeth and breathed shallowly on the 15-degree hillside slope where the tractor might hold but the disc was forever slipping sideways and menacing the downhill vines.

"That can be a half-gallon hill," said Allan Nelson, who had worked it for years before me.

"A half-gallon hill?" I asked in bafflement.

"Yes," he said. "A man might drink a half-gallon of wine at lunch after he comes off it."

Allan can afford to comfort others with his humor, for he is a tractor artist. With a disc behind a Caterpillar, he can take tractor, disc, drag and roller, all twenty-four feet of clattering, unjointed metal, out of one row and into another in one carved sweep at full throttle.

"The secret to getting through it fast," he once told me, "is to spend as little time as possible on the headlands. You aren't doing any good out there; so get out and back in fast."

Other men can learn to do it, but Allan has a flair that catches the eye. My crew and I stopped work unbidden one day when he was working down the weeds in an orchard across the road and the steady roar of his tractor engine suddenly dropped. One blade of his front gang was stopped just short of hooking into a tree trunk. He backed once, then took off again at full throttle, and the whole train of metal, once twitched into the proper angle, curved around the threatened trunk and back into a straight pull, leaving not enough space between the blades and the tree to see.

There are men who can do that almost without

looking, men who take one tractor through a whole season without a breakdown. There are others who have five tractors for two drivers and yet are always fixing something, who seem to be steadily swearing as they charge down each row. However, for an example of the pure *tao* of tractor work, I have not yet met the equal of my neighbor to the north, Richard Mounts.

Richard is a young man whose entire broad frame gives an impression of deliberate, steady strength. He has trained to a lifetime of farming and has kept a dry wit that can play successfully with visiting intellectuals. He is not a Renaissance man, but a successful farmer with no apologies to give.

On groundworking days, Richard is out of his small, white house next to Dry Creek by seven. He drives up the hill in his carefully kept World War II jeep, carrying water in a big, round canteen covered with blanket material that cools by evaporation. At his equipment barn he services a big, green, four-wheel-drive tractor, adjusts the disc for the soil he is about to work, then starts out deliberately and takes it row by row, hour by hour, at a steady three miles per hour.

If his concentration fades, Richard does not shake his head, grit his teeth and push on. He stops, swings off the tractor, unslings the canteen, takes a drink or two, caps the canteen slowly, then swings back aboard. If the disc sinks into wet ground, he gets off and without hurry unhitches the disc, goes to the front of the tractor and unwinds the chain wreathed carefully about the front-end weights, hitches the chain to the disc and drives the tractor off to dry ground. Then he hitches chain to tractor and twitches the disc out of the mud, gets off, recouples the implement, stows all his gear and goes on.

Hour after hour, Richard goes on. He takes an hour for lunch. He stops before sunset to refuel. Day after droning day, Richard Mounts gets through it. In 1980, after all, we all did.

The rain returned on the ninth of that April and

The main irrigation pump, heart of the frost protection system, being reinstalled just as the willows leaf out in spring.

again on the twentieth, as if it had been ordered in to wet down the dead weeds and speed their rotting away and also to turn back the clock on our ten-minute ground. Still, it had been a rush.

I started dusting the vineyard with mineral sulfur for the first time at three in the morning on April 30, at least ten days later than would have been best to get the sulfur out and fuming on the leaves, where the fumes fill the nose for the rest of the growing season. Fuming sulfur is applied to kill powdery mildew before it gets a dirty grey hold on leaves or grapes. I confessed to Gene Cuneo that I was two dustings behind, at least.

"Don't you know?" he asked. "We're always behind, all of us. Come on, now, you wouldn't know how to live any more than we do if you ever got ahead."

A grape grower loads his power duster with powdered mineral sulfur to be blown into the vines by the fan at the back of the duster.

The first stage of tillage
completed.

CHAPTER SIX

The Grand Period of Growth

On a certain spring day every year in our vineyards, the accumulating weight of hundreds of fragments of work done day by day, for more than a month, all seems to slide into place at once and fit together for a clear and perfect purpose. This sudden coalescing yields one long moment of exhilaration. That morning, the air is as clear and tasty as if it had been poured all night from a crystal cup. At least for that day, which has no fixed date, the cold sting is gone from the predawn darkness and warmth grows steadily with the sun. The vines stand with every green shoot upraised, and the first hour of sunlight pours through the whole length of each of those shoots, turning them all into translucent green wands. After a stuttering start stretching over four weeks or more, the shoots are about three feet long by that poised moment. They reach skyward like arms upraised in joy. For rows on end, all equally green and without blemish, the

The tip of a vine shoot in the grand period of growth.

vines and perfect shoots go on, and a farmer is tempted to imagine that they all are lined up that morning to raise silent hosannas in thanks for battles won and growing done.

On that day in late April or early May, everything seems possible. There are no signs of disease or infestation. The vines are strong and sound. They look capable of anything: of setting a perfect bumper crop, of commanding a princely price, of retiring the mortgage in one year. On that day the dust lies down and the disc runs true; no hoses snap and no pieces drop; engines start and pumps suck. Even the dogs may catch a rabbit.

The vines, on that spring day, have already begun what viticultural textbooks call the grand period of growth. Very softly, they tick and rustle in that morning's sun, whispering with no wind. I have never found the precise source of those tiny vineyard sounds on wholly still mornings, but I know that they come from the vines without any stirring wind and that I only hear them during this grand period. I have come to imagine that the vines might be creaking internally with effort, because they are about to push their shoots through most of the year's growth in about three weeks. It is as though they had waited until conditions of sunlight, air and soil temperature were just right. Now, they seem to decide, we can do all the growing a tidy and circumspect grapevine might need. In the days that follow that magic morning, every year, a farmer can often measure by eye the growth at the shoot tips from morning to evening. Those tips stretch up and out so fast that he can almost stop to watch them grow.

The grand period of growth, following that morning on which the vines seem to rise in their rows and give a glad shout, establishes the living structure for that year's crop and begins building buds for the next. Little embryonic grapes in limp clusters have been visible at the base of each fruitful shoot since the second week after budbreak. Now, in the few weeks before those tiny, green embryos flower and form grapes, all the bones, sinews and leafy organs that will carry the crop and ripen it grow out and stand ready. If one thinks of the grapevines as seventh-graders, it is as though they were to jump though puberty and adolescence, complete college, marry and have their first children, all in the compass of one long spring vacation. And, after his one morning moment of joy, the prospect of that growth spurt into bloom pushes the grape grower into his final spring frenzy.

The day of the glad shout in 1980 was April 29, but my field log does not record any pause for reverence:

Tuesday, April 29. Low 35°. Clear hot. 0730–1630 Miguel, Juan, Jesse, Ausilio & Jorge sucker/hoe house hill. 0730–1600 JN disc help hill.

By then, the weather had put even the best and wisest farmers behind schedule. On that morning, the first one suitable for sulfur dusting after a spell of wet weather that went dry with windy days and nights, the yellowish white clouds behind dusting tractors at dawn wound like sandy worm trails through the green hillside vineyards and billowed into the air like rooster tails above the flats. On that night and the next, we all were out powdering the vines with sulfur dust and filling the valley with the sound of tractor engines and the deep, windy hum of dusting machines, which use fans to drive the dust in clouds up into all the seams and curls of new leaves and tendrils. We need to cover every bit of growing surface with a light dusting of sulfur, and keep all covered until growth stops, to prevent mildew.

We work at night because it is the only time there is no wind to carry the dust away from the vines, and because dew forming after midnight on their growing parts helps the dust settle and stick. The ex-urbanites who have moved to wine county for its tranquility, and who make three-hour commutes away from it each day, hate the practice. In St. Helena, a posh little town near the head of the Napa Valley, there was recently a citizens' attempt to stop all sulfur dusting in the surrounding vineyards, on the grounds that mineral sulfur borne downwind into town might eat away the rubber of swimming pool covers. Here, and in St. Helena, the enemies of night dusting seem to resent most the loss of their sleep. They have not yet grown numerous enough to shift top priority away from farming in the agricultural countryside they covet.

We are regularly warned that those who want farmers, in these desirable countrysides near large cities, turned into groundskeepers who will tend, noiselessly and without odors or trucks, everyone's green view are going to outnumber us soon. However, particularly in May with bloom on the way, a man does not have time to stop and worry about that possibility.

There is worrying enough to be done about keeping machinery together, about getting through it and about getting all the modern chemical spells in place on time to do the most good. A grower must now keep up his dusting every ten days. He must get preventive sprays on the vineyard just before and just at bloom. He should watch the vines for lack of water and oversee his crews as they peel unfruitful shoots off each vine by hand. He must keep up the rhythm of groundwork. It is enough.

Thinning unwanted growth in the vineyard is called

suckering, and it is simple but painstaking. At its easiest, suckering means pulling off and discarding every shoot that shows no grape clusters and getting all of these off before they have had time to draw too much of the vine's stored energy away from the fruitful shoots. There are subtleties, however, that may involve attempts to control the crop load, to let only the strongest fruitful shoots keep growing, or attempts to reshape the vine by allowing a nonfruitful shoot to grow and become a bearing spur in the following year. Therefore, a grower has either to trust the men and women suckering for him or he has to sucker with them. In either case, he must watch closely.

Still, for me at least, suckering is a human job, done with hands and mind, and is not as frustrating as any of the prebloom tasks that a grower must do with his machines. Farm machinery, which looks so powerful and full of purpose, can be deceptive.

A visiting friend, an accomplished correspondent for an East Coast newspaper with several novels to his credit, once became practically rhapsodic as he described my bright red wheel tractor to me. While the tractor stood unresponsive over a puddle of its own hydraulic oil in the barnyard, my friend Bill said that farm machinery is good and true. He pointed out the absence of fins and chrome, which make cars such misleading creations; he talked about the simplicity of design and the power of line.

"That tractor is nothing more than it shows you," he said. "It is its job and it does its job."

Perhaps. Perhaps, also, beauty not only lies in the eye of the beholder but can take up residence inside the beholder's eye, blocking his view. As Bill talked about the absence of ornamentation, I could only think of the thirty minutes it took me to undo and refasten the red sheet metal cap screwed over the engine, in order to replace the fuel gauge wire that was forever drifting off its simple connections. When he spoke of simplicity of design, I could only remember how the factory's adaptation of that tractor model for close-quarters vineyard work had set the rear wheels so close together that only Houdini could have con-

veniently mounted any of the portable implements normally carried on a tractor's rear-facing arms. Anyone else was in for a long, repetitive tussle.

Furthermore, a design and manufacturing mistake in the steering had severely handicapped that tractor on the job. It would not track true on a paved highway. It hopped and hitched its wandering way between vine rows and kept any driver's adrenalin level constantly high. In defense of Bill's view, he might say such a defect was a blessing in that it would always keep me awake. It did that, but so does the true-tracking tractor for which I finally traded the wandering one. This one is underpowered, in my view, and Bill would certainly say that my jaundiced view blocks my perception of its beauty.

That may well be, but I know I am not alone among farmers in hating sprayers. Sprayers, at least the ones I have known, are the Rube Goldberg jokes in a grape grower's mechanical menagerie. Basically, they consist only of a tank in which to mix that day's poisons, a pump to suck in the poison mix and discharge it, under pressure, through nozzles that turn the mix to mist, a fan to blow the mist about with a gale-force artificial wind and the pipes, belts and controls to put the parts together. However, they seem to have been designed by Murphy's simple-minded cousin, who did not grasp that his cousin's law was a warning to thoughtful design engineers to foresee what might go wrong. The cousin in charge of sprayers instead set out to prove that, indeed, anything that can go wrong, will.

It may be my dislike of the work we have to do together that makes me and the sprayer enemies. I will confess that I sweat inside the respirator protecting me from the pesticides that I must mix and spray. My face plate fogs. I cringe slightly sometimes, as I drive down the rows, waiting for one of the tangle of pressurized hoses behind me to burst and bathe me in the concentrated stuff.

Still, my fear is founded. Sprayer hoses do unpredictably pop off their fittings. Strainers routinely clog and nozzles block. Belts slip and the pressure varies so that application is unexpectedly uneven. Bearings do work out of alignment. In fact, I have seen another, normally taciturn farmer, a man who made part of his living spraying for others with the same new make and model I use, bouncing on his toes with anger at the dealer's parts counter as he told the rest of us, waiting there for bits or pieces to fix broken machines, that his sprayer had chewed up two new complete sets of fan drive belts in as many days at ninety dollars per set. Sprayers are not, on balance, congenial machines, and so most Dry Creek Valley grape growers seem to avoid using them unless they must.

For example, instead of spraying as a matter of annual routine to kill the little, white flies called grape leafhoppers, a grower can count them as they hatch, consult a table and decide whether there are enough to outlive their natural predators and do what the table calls "economically significant damage." If not, the grower need not spray. He can hold off spraying for thrips, also, and gamble that rising temperature will hold them in check.

I tend to leave leafhopper and thrip control to their natural enemies, if I can, but I grow no grapes worth more than $450 per ton. If I did, I might be more inclined to buy pesticides and bet their cost against slightly higher yields. If I did that, however, I might open the door for further chemical costs, because spraying for thrips or leafhoppers early in the season also kills their insect enemies and may clear the field for a later infestation of other grape pests. This kind of blind choice, full of unknowns in the conditional tense, is typical of those that a grape grower must make at every stage of each growing season. To make them, farming instinct based on many growing seasons works best. To get more than just one, individual share of experience from each growing season, farmers everywhere talk a lot of shop. Over coffee at the doughnut shop, at the parts store and by the side of the road, stubbing their toes reflectively into the dirt, farmers exchange a lot of long, detailed and circumstantial descriptions of what has been happening to them. These conversations while kicking at clods sound awfully windy to outsiders, about as windy, say, as a graduate seminar on production management techniques for extruded

plastic containers or on estate tax planning. They all, I believe, serve the same purpose.

A few choices are purely economical, even with pesticides. For example, there are fungicides that, to be effective, must be applied long before the rot-producing fungus is visible. Almost all grape growers use them to kill botrytis spores that almost certainly land on the vines' flowers as they are becoming grapes.

Getting these fungicides on at one precise moment during bloom is imperative if a grower wants to have some insurance against botrytis spores growing out of the grapes months later, should the grape skins split after a harvesttime rain. Under those far-off conditions, the moldy grey rot the spores produce might ruin a crop in three days. So he adjusts the sprayer for that, at the very least, and waits for bloom.

> Tuesday, May 13. Low 40°. High clouds. 0730–1630 Angel, Jose Luis, Concepcion sucker Zins. Miguel, Juan, Jesse, Ausilio, Jorge sucker Carignane. One-hour lunch. Began final pass disc on flat. Early warning vines show bloom.

Wine grapes are formed in a blooming process, although it is almost invisible. Like apple trees, peaches, pears and prunes, they blossom, but they do so almost secretively and without any aerial display of flowers. The grape flower, which has been maturing since just after budbreak, has no petals but a little, green cap of tissue, called a calyptra, that peels open from the bottom up, then pops off. These flowers, on the eve of bloom, look like tiny, green replicas of slightly puckered mature grapes. When blossoming begins, the green cap goes, and one morning, where it had been, there are four white stamens standing in the air like stiff bits of thread, with just the barest touch of yellow pollen at their anther tips. It looks as though some very small sea anemones had moved onto the nascent grape clusters overnight.

The process is so private a grower could almost miss it in the rush, but there is one silent signal when bloom is underway. The flowering grapes yield a faint and delicate sweet smell, just strong enough to catch at human nostrils but not powerful enough to mean much to bees. As best the plant physiologists have been able to tell, grapevines cross-pollinate their own flowers, with what I would call quite characteristic discretion, and with little or no help from bees.

> Friday, May 16. Low 38°. Clear to high clouds. 0730–1630 Miguel, Juan, Jesse, Ausilio, Jorge finish sucker Gamay. Angel, Jose Luis, Concepcion sucker Zins; almost done. Paid. Some Carignane, some Colombard bloom.

The rule governing bloom that was passed down in the Dry Creek Valley from its first Italian grape growers was: "Don't even walk through the vineyard during bloom."

However, research conducted since 1930 has not substantiated any reason why farmers should keep out of their vineyards during the two or three weeks when their wine grapes are in flower. So, we all tend to go racketing through the vineyards on our normal business, getting through it if we can. The only interferences with normal flowering that have been clearly identified are heavy rain, which swells up and bursts the pollen grains, and daytime cold below 68 degrees, or heat above 95 degrees, in the vineyard, when the grapes, quite sensibly, stop blooming.

Months later, at harvest, when the wine pundits say whether it has been a good year or bad for wine in California, they can point to a heat wave or to cold, rainy weather at bloom time if they choose to call the year not good. Those two, along with frosts at budbreak, a cool summer, a cold autumn or rains at harvest are clear and un-controversial culprits for anything less than California's usual good growing fortune. The case against a hard, steady wind at bloom is not so technically clear, but, here on the ground, we call it bad.

> Wednesday, May 21. Low 44°. Clear. 0700–1200. Start bunch rot control. Spray N. end Colombard. Break-downs, hoses, everything. Good weather until noon, when hard NW came in.

That hard northwest wind, which pours in a dry storm off the Pacific at least once each spring as California's interior valleys first heat up to summer temperature levels, is never wholly welcome. Early in the spring, it can help dry out soggy soil, but it also can dry the ground quickly past the ten-minute point. The wind can dissipate humid warmth in the air when the shoots are growing fast and are most vulnerable to fungus infection, but it also can break those same tender shoots right off the vines of some varieties. During bloom, at the very least, northwest wind gusting to gale force day and night can keep a man from spraying when he must. At its worst, it can drop the temperature steeply and blow pollen away.

> Friday, May 23. Low 45°. Clear. High wind overnight. 0600–1430 Miguel, Juan, Ausilio hoe east hill. <u>Bad bloom conditions.</u> Breakdown vines.

> Saturday, May 24. Low 44°. Clear, cold. High wind. No help. Paid. Bloom stopped—or almost. There will be uneven ripening.

The heavy, black underlining in my field log scored the paper, but it did not stop the northwest wind. The wind blew for five bad-tempered days, past the optimum point for spraying fungicides on four or five varieties of grapes. Vines at the weather edges of the most susceptible vineyards in the valley looked as though they had been mauled by vandals. Their four-foot-long shoots, broken off where they had sprung from the limbs, dragged alongside, dying quickly in the dirt.

CHAPTER SEVEN

"You All Caught Up?"

Serenity settles slowly over a vineyard after the grapes for that year's wine have blossomed. A kind of peace returns, at the same gentle pace with which the growing shoots slowly harden into canes, bend with their own weight, bow down and finally join at their still-growing tips across the open ground between vine rows. As the canes grow longer and curve into the shape of low waterfalls, the pace and purpose of vineyard work changes too.

The threat of frost is gone. The willows are growing hard and all the swallows have nested. The late-comers among them are forced to crowd and jostle one another in the last dwindling puddles in the valley to pack their beaks with building mud. The peregrine falcons pass in pairs down the valley, hunting as they fly from their nesting trees on the highlands north of us. At the same time, as the days stretch out and grow steadily hotter, the local animals and migratory birds

The first pause in tractor work.

that stop here settle into familiar quarters and established seasonal routines, like summer residents returning to a resort town. Deer that have wintered in the green hills drop down each evening into the vineyards nearest those hills, where both water and forage are now drying up, to feed on the green growing tips of vine canes. White herons return in a flock and fly up and down Dry Creek, searching out hunting pools that will hold water and fish through the wholly dry summer. Rain after April is a rarity in our wine-growing climate, and rain after May is a downright oddity. Dry Creek turns true to its name by July or August, and the sun bleaches its gravel bars to a dusty grey. Suckers, chub and trapped trout hide in the weedy corners of the cold pools that remain, and any animal that depends on water must stake its claims early. The tall blue heron who roosts near our house each summer and stalks the little creek that runs through the vineyards until it, too, dries up, leaves every morning on slow wings and returns in the dusk. On those late-May days when the temperature first reaches above 90 degrees here, he may return early and stand motionless through the middle of the day against the creek bank on a bend where the shade is deepest.

Tracks in the dust on newly dry farm roads show that skunks, possums and raccoons have been hunting silently at night; but the barn owls advertise that they are abroad, hooting like ghosts floating through the tree lines. The silent coveys in which quail spend the winter together break up when the adults nest in pairs, but the separated birds call to one another in the evening, perhaps in order to stay in touch.

Suddenly noticing again the details of natural life in and around the vineyard is an annual sign, I believe, of a change in a grower's vision that matches the change in the needs of his grapes. The flowing year has made its second turn, the first since the dormant buds opened two months earlier. A crop is on the vines, and the current of the growing season slows down. So, eventually, does the grape grower. This yoked-together change in pace is signaled to me when my vision of the vineyard expands beyond the mechanical chore immediately at hand, which has been so important as to fill my foreground every day for weeks on end, and I begin again to notice the deer, the herons and the nesting quail. To Richard Mounts, the farmer with the steadiest tractor pace in the neighborhood, the change to a closer, more considered view seems to announce itself in the same way.

"There are days in spring when the fog lifts early but sort of sticks on my hill there," he told me. We were standing on a very favored spot on Richard's land, where three gentle planted slopes come together in a curving swale, and looking south and west at the forested green wall of Dry Creek Valley only a few hundred yards away. "Patches of it hang in the trees and stream up the swales while the sun is burning through. You've seen it.

"I tell you," Richard said, "I'll stop the tractor for five or ten minutes at a time just to sit and watch those hills."

Another young man, of the third generation in his family born and bred to dirt farming, told me that this moment in the year, above all others, is the time to talk to the vines. Knowing that it is now time to talk to his vines represents the way the change in the year's pace is signaled to him.

"Man who doesn't talk to his vines," said this very matter-of-fact farmer, "won't have any idea what they're going to do."

Until I heard that from him, some years ago, I had thought I might be the only farmer hereabouts who did talk to his grapevines: asking them how they felt, reassuring them when some particular pest had moved in or thanking them when they had carried themselves through some bad patch. Now, I suspect many of us do that.

Certainly, the days just after the grapes bloom are one time when talking to the vines comes naturally, as a part of the business at hand. Each vine has become an individual again, resolving out of the green blur that has been streaming past the tractor on both sides for four weeks. A grower peers inside his vines on business over and over again. He parts the canes and turns leaves, searching for signs of illness. He counts insects. He examines his new grapes, which look now, at birth, like hard, deep green BBs stuck to the very tips of rubbery, light green stalks that have grown into a pattern reminiscent of a rib cage. These loose bunches-to-be, called clusters at this time in their lives, hang limply in pairs at the base of each cane. They are the heart of the vineyard, but they are extremely unprepossessing. They look tentative and frail, as if they were exhausted and unprepared for all the growing left to do. Indeed, in all growing years, some grapes will simply drop off their vines at this point in a natural crop-thinning process known, quite graphically, as shattering.

Around the dangling clusters, though, life is robust. A farmer on his first inspection will find that whole microcosms have settled and grown in the shifting green light beneath the vine leaves while he was not looking. Birds will have nested there, and, quite often during this first round of close inspections, little cups of woven grass turn up, their

The high atmospheric
pressure that keeps California
summers dry holds the smoke
from burning vineyard brush
in still layers.

bare eggs a reproach to the man who has frightened off the brooding mother. Spiders will have spun pretty patterns while casting their webs into the oddly angled corners formed by canes and limbs and vine trunks. A grower focuses more closely still. He is looking now for minuscule signs of how the life inside each vine is balanced. He examines leaves in order to discover whether vine-eating insects and their natural predators have established an equilibrium. A tiny red insect, no bigger than a spot of cayenne pepper, streaking on six invisible legs across a green leaf surface is a good sign. That insect is a mite, and it eats other mites too small to see. The smaller mites feed, very injuriously, on vine leaves.

Grape leafhopper eggs, injected just under the surface on the undersides of leaves and now swollen to the size and shape of very small grains of rice, are not good signs. But a farmer must look more closely still. Are all the eggs white, or do a noticeable number look orange? An orange cast inside an egg shows that a tiny wasp, visible only with a magnifying glass, has found the leafhopper egg and used it as food for its own brood—fortunately for the farmer and fatally for that hopper. That one will die in the egg and never grow up to suck food from the leaves and fly off the vines with its tiny fellows in an irritating white swarm. If there is an apparent balance between vine eaters and the insects that eat them, a grower can sigh and let both live, and—great news—give up using the sprayer again for that year.

A vineyard-wide inspection is one on a list of jobs postponed daily through the spring rush, chores such as fixing a leaky hydraulic control valve or changing a fan belt, which become possible now in the little lull that comes just after bloom. In the lull, growers are waiting to see how many of the tiny, green grapes will drop off their skeleton clusters and how many will stay on to swell and ripen.

There is a standard farmer's greeting—"You all caught up?"—that turns up often hereabouts just at this time of year and could almost serve to label the lull at this turning point. "You all caught up?" a friend from across the creek will ask when you run across each other in front of the parts counter at the tractor dealer. The proper response lies somewhere between "No way" and "Gettin' there," because a farmer is never entirely caught up. There is always a residual list of things to be done soon. Jobs waiting their turn for attention move up to greet any farmer as soon as the uppermost on his list are crossed off.

After bloom in 1980, one of the tasks that forced itself to the top of that list on my place was dealing with the sadness of Ausilio Torres. Ausilio is a small, strong man with gentle ways who had lived on the place and worked with me for several years. He was well into his fifties, a family man with grown sons also working in the vineyards, and well and widely known, with affection, in the Mexican community of the region. He drank, moderately, with men of his own age on his days off, but Ausilio was also a favorite with much younger men working in the fields. They had given him his nickname, Chilo, an affectionate contraction. A widowed lady from town who drove around the valley vineyards collecting beer cans and bottles from the help houses for paid recycling always asked for Don Ausilio here and, if she found him in, stayed talking for hours, although Ausilio never invited her in nor ever, that I saw, offered to drive on with her.

After the harvest of 1979, Ausilio Torres had made his farewells to me with a short, formal speech and a tearful *abrazo*. He had returned, with his two eldest sons, to his native town in Mexico. They had accomplished what they had come north to do and returned almost in triumph, taking with them a solid, used pickup and their own rebuilt tractor to work their thirty acres in Guanajuato and to hire out to unmechanized neighbors. In December the news came from Mexico that Humberto Torres, the second son, had been shot dead at point-blank range there by another young man who had worked in northern California at about the same time as the Torres family. He had been known here as the "Willits Killer."

No one knew why he had shot twenty-year-old Humberto. There had been no known argument, no bad blood that anyone could recall, and the Willits Killer had

Above: Birds nest in some vines each year, and their families grow as the grapes begin to swell.

Left: A summer spider web, stretched in the air between the growing vines.

fled. The Torres family, of course, had sworn vengeance, but they couldn't find the other man and could not interest the local prosecutor in pursuing him.

One wet day in April, Ausilio returned. He stood in the drizzle outside my door with his wide-brimmed hat of tightly woven white straw tilted back, and he smiled and said very little. It was Miguel Silva, who called Ausilio "Uncle" but was, by strict American accounting, a young second cousin, who stood at his side and explained that Ausilio was back and looking for work and a place to live. He was welcome to move back in and share the house with the two Silva brothers, my steady hired help. By Mexican accounting, the two were his nephews and owed him deference and obedience.

Ausilio smiled. He declined an invitation to come in and warm up with a glass of brandy. He kept smiling when I expressed my formal sympathy for his loss, but his eyes filled with tears. On the next dry day he was back at work,

Burning dried piles of hand-cleared puncture vine, one of a grape grower's summer chores.

as steady and as silent as before, but now withdrawn and un-laughing. So it went, uncharacteristically, through the steady work of stripping off unfruitful shoots. When the work slacked off, the Silva brothers came to ask me for help. They were worried. Their uncle, they said, had been drinking himself to sleep almost every night of the week. He would not, they said, listen to two near-nephews.

"And that Jesse helps him buy the beer and drinks it with him," Miguel said. "You talk to my Uncle Chilo; we cannot."

Jesse was a man of Ausilio's height and age with hard hands and a seamed face that turned weak about the eyes. He had been hired to help after the creek bank washed out and had stayed on to sucker. He worked quickly, did only what was required and took his payday pleasures where he most easily could buy them. Jesse, whose given name was Ernesto Rodriguez, was a solitary; a man who in an earlier time in California would have been known as a professional farmhand, a wanderer. Before tackling Jesse, I talked to Ausilio about the drinking, but it did no apparent good. Ausilio worked steadily but barely talked during the day. He took to standing still, as if at a loss for a moment, when time was called for a break, or at lunch or the end of the day. It was as if his concentration could last only as long as it was tightly tied to a single task.

So after bloom I talked to Jesse. He followed, smiling, my explanation of Ausilio's need for tranquility, rest and nights without beer, but looked at me throughout with unsmiling eyes.

"Tell you what, I'll go," he said. "I can find another job. But I think you're seeing it wrong. Ausilio is man enough to decide what he wants, and I don't make him drink. I keep him company, which is more than I can say for the nephews."

Clearly, there was dissension at the help house. Equally clearly, Ausilio, who had no head for liquor in the best of times, was handling his grief with bottles and cans. Perhaps that would pass, I thought, if he were to be without a drinking companion and were to feel that he must set an example for his two nephews. I apologized but agreed that Jesse leave. It was time to get back into the vineyard. There was work still to do before the vines grew fully closed across their rows.

> Friday, June 6. Clear. Variable winds. Warming. 0600–1430 Miguel, Juan, Ausilio hoe out sprinkler rows. Half-hour lunch. 0300–0800 JN dust flat every row.

After the lull, too, a grape grower can count the hard, green berries that have stuck on his clusters and make an estimate of what the crop in each block of vineyard may be. The estimate is no more than that. Even if I had counted every bunch of unripe grapes on each of the 41,833 vines I was farming, I could not have foretold my final delivered tonnage with accuracy. However, there is a statistical sampling technique, based on counting unripe grapes in clusters on representative vines in each block, that has been worked out by the excellent viticultural farm advisors who work in California vineyards as agents of the University of California Cooperative Extension Service. This technique, although it amounts to little more than a guess set in numbers, is reassuringly technical and at least helps to figure the odds for some of the choices that must be made after the crop is, as farmers say, "set."

The vineyard crop is set when the BB-size berries no longer drop off their bunches if shaken and when they begin to grow toward their final shape. The grapes began to swell in Dry Creek Valley that year in June, slightly late but nonetheless in good time to provide pondering room for the next set of farmer's choices.

Should a grower spray at this point, before the vines close across the rows, for whatever insects he has seen in his vineyard, or should he let stand the natural balance and take his chances that it will hold? If he waits until later, tractors pulling sprayers will unavoidably damage vines.

Where will he water and when?

And, above all, should he thin out the crop on his vines to make sure it will ripen in what is left of the year?

This last is the most enigmatic of the late-spring decisions because it necessarily balances what a grower can guess about the size of the crop against what he cannot know about the weather in August and September, the ripening months, and about how choosy his winery will turn out to be when the harvest deliveries of grapes begin.

These choices are what the extension agents, kind folks all, call "management decisions." The euphemism has a soothing sound and reassuring overtones of command, control or at least management of the factors before the manager. However, it is axiomatic that no farmer can control or even manage the major factors affecting his crop: the weather and the market.

Take, for example, the vineyard manager's yearly choice about irrigation in the vineyards north of San Francisco. If he waters once in a dry June, and July is hot, the manager may be tempted to invest in the cost of another irrigation in late July, when the grapes turn color, because the second watering will keep his grapes plump. Plump grapes weigh more, and wine grapes are bought by the ton.

What, then, if August is cool and the rain returns in September instead of in October or November? The water-plump grapes, still unripe after a cool August, will split in the September rains and start to rot. Part of the crop may be lost outright, and much of it may prove unacceptable to the winery that buys the manager's grapes.

And what if he doesn't water the second time, and August proves hot and September dry? The grapes will wither in the heat and can lose 30 percent of their weight in a few days when they are ready for harvesting. A 30 percent weight loss means a drop of 30 percent in the payment the grower will receive for that crop, the only payment he will get for one year's work.

"I don't see why anyone in this valley would ever pay to go to Reno," one of my neighbors with forty years of experience as a farmer's wife says every time she hears the debate over such choices get technical. "Farmers are the biggest gamblers there are."

There are farming decisions to be made to get the most out of the natural magic going on every year in a vineyard, but most of them seem to come up in the form of quick and instinctive choices, like the head fakes and stutter steps of a broken field runner. Carefully made plans, calculated and costed out to a nicety, seem always to need changing to fit the momentary changes in the field. In a culture under the sign of the computer, all farmers seem to feel a little uneasy with instinctive choices made on the run. We prefer to think of ourselves as fundamentally managers. Fortunately for our self-esteem, there are fine-line distinctions to be made that affect the costs of carrying out choices whose final outcome remains in the lap of the gods. On these budgeting decisions, at least, a man can bring to bear what farmers, too, call a "sharp pencil." Calculating how much one alternative should cost and how much more it might bring in can be done, and it is much more reassuring than to punch in for work every day as an instinctive gambler.

In June of 1980, my sharp pencil said I had spent more through bloom than I had the year before. The national minimum wage had increased by law, and I had raised field wages to stay slightly ahead of the requirement. Also, there had been the unforseen expense of repairing the creek bank and rebuilding the main pump connections. Like any other farmer, I could then add in my anticipated remaining costs before harvest. In the case of my vineyard, these were the cost of irrigations to come, foreseeable overhead expenses and property taxes. I calculated that my crop costs that year probably would total close to $895 per acre, before one grape was picked. Harvest costs are hard to foretell.

Later that year our extension agents published vineyard cost and investment figures for the business in 1980. Picking through their tables, it seems that my farming practices up to harvest should have cost $904 per acre. Since the two figures are so close, I venture to offer the following table of expenses, gross income from grape sales and mortgage payments as a kind of broad-brush outline of the economics of wine grape growing. The brush is very broad, but I believe this table fairly well represents the case of the small, independent vineyard owner-operator who sells his grapes to a winery he does not own.

THE GROSS ECONOMICS OF WINE GRAPE GROWING
Costs and Revenues per Acre

	1979	1980	1979	1980
Gross grape income			$1805	$2034
Costs to ripeness	$1016	$ 895		
Insurance and reserve for contingencies		105		
Harvest	192	210		
Cost to produce			1208	1210
Net before banks			597	824
Mortgage payments: land, buildings, vines, stakes, irrigation, equipment			650	710
Profit (loss)			($ 53)	$ 114

The figures for 1979, a good year, were in the books. The 1980 gross income estimate was based on my count of immature grape bunches, but I could not know the price they would fetch when ripe. Like the majority of California grape growers, I had always learned the price to be paid for my grapes after they had been grown, ripened, picked, delivered and made into wine. Each year's price had been announced to most of us by a check sent from the purchasing winery months after the growing year was over. That is the way the purchase of wine grapes has been handled except where growers have managed to negotiate and sign contracts with the wineries that will buy their grapes. Contracts have been the exception, rather than the rule, in all but a few of California's wine-grape-growing regions.

Of course, mine was the hopeful view of the man on the ground; so I used the prices that had been paid by the winery in 1979. I used them to decide, then, that thinning out the crop set on ten acres of Zinfandel by pulling off bunches by hand could, might–no, should–pay off. However, any outsider reading that table of my penciled estimates would have looked past the middle lines, where the choices lay, to the bottom lines. He might, no doubt, have been shocked at how bad the grape business looked for anyone trying to use it to pay off a mortgage. In self-defense, I could say that the extention service figures made wine grape farming look even worse.

Take away the mortgage payments from my table, and even a blunt pencil would show an improved bottom line to anyone interested in raising grapes for a living. With the debt service removed, still the return on an investment in grape farming was very low for those years of rising interest rates. A statewide peak of a 2 percent return to capital invested in wine grape growing was considered good, in 1979, by extension service economists.

Both the extension service figures and mine made it clear why established grape growers, those who owned their acreage, equipment, irrigation systems and buildings largely free of debt, could hold onto their vineyards with some confidence. Like any gambler, they might look forward to good years and bad. Unlike the mortgaged farmer, they could reasonably expect to weather the bad ones. However, it had already become clear in wine country by 1980 that the only people who could afford to step into the vineyard business as newcomers were those who could pay for their farming debt with other incomes.

By that year, wine grape farming had become a rich man's game. New vineyard owners in all the sought-after lands north of San Francisco were, most typically: doctors, lawyers, dentists, oil men, entertainers, airline pilots, highly paid executives or engineers who had sold small, valuable technical businesses. Almost all left the farming work to hired local managers and their crews. Now that is a true management decision. It makes quite direct economic sense for an owner to pay someone else an annual salary of $7,500 or even $16,000, then the going rate for a full-time vineyard manager in northern Sonoma County, to run his vineyard when he will make a quarter of a million dollars in that same year and his vineyard is losing money. It would make no economic sense to give up his high salary and work full time to replace a $16,000-a-year farmer. And every dollar of operating loss represents a tax loss for the high-income owner in his high tax bracket. Yet many of the

dollars thus "lost" might represent improvements to the owner's property.

Anyone with an oil well, according to one local quip, could buy and support a vineyard. But for how long? There was another quip, more cautionary for the new vineyardists, that had already begun to make the rounds then.

"A vineyard," the second quip ran, "is a good way to make a small fortune out of a large one."

The Russian River in an early summer sunset.

CHAPTER EIGHT

Coasting

The parts of the year have special names in every farming region, names that are specific to the place, its crops and to the way that the seasons show their changes in that place. These names are a way of telling the times of the year by the most telling event, for farmers, in each one. In California's North Coast vineyard country, the calendar year begins with pruning, but the first season with its own name is "frost," when the growing year begins. After "frost" comes "bloom," when the crop is set. But summer has no name.

Thinking back, a farmer in the Dry Creek Valley will naturally place local events he may remember in their proper time of year by using the familiar local names for seasons. I have heard a man recall, for example, that tragedy struck a family living on his place with an automobile wreck that happened during "frost." Summer now is just plain "summer" here. It was not always so.

A vineyard must be watered often in its first summer.

When the valley floor was covered with orchards, before the vineyards pushed them out, "apples" and "pears," depending on which fruit a farmer grew, were the names for August, the month when picking began. "Pears" was followed by "prunes" on the local calendar in the years when the September opening of public schools was delayed until after the prune harvest was complete, so that schoolchildren could help with picking and drying. Farmers and their families finished "prunes" and usually were "in grapes," as their expression then went, by October. "Grapes," then, became a useful name for autumn.

Now there are no apples, very few pears and only scattered acres of prune orchards. Only one harvest remains that involves us all, the grape picking that begins in late August to mid-September and can last into November. That part of the year has become known as "harvest," and July and August slip past without a farming name to tell them by.

July is a balancing point in the year, when the fatigue held at bay for four months seems to sag down and settle on a grower for a while. His grapes are growing bigger, filling up the bunches and standing proud beneath the leaves, but they are still wholly green and almost as hard as almonds. There is watering to be done, irrigations just finishing or being taken up for the second time, but they only involve turning pumps on and off or, at worst, carrying thirty-foot lengths of movable pipe overhead above the vines twice each day for an hour or two, in the cool hours at dawn and at dusk. Sulfur dusting must be kept up. After watering, too, it is good to pull something through the vineyard behind the tractor that will nip off the weed seedlings between the vine rows. Still, a farmer can rest because, except in unusual years, there is time in hand.

Time shows in the way we talk about work. In most months of the year, if someone asks a farmer how it's going, usually he will not answer, "Fine," particularly to another farmer. Rather, he will respond with an estimate of how far along he is in the common tasks of the month.

If I meet a friend in town in January, for example, and ask, "How're you doing?" he may say, "All right. We've got eighty acres pruned and twenty-some to go. And you?"

In July, if I meet the same friend and ask how he's doing, likely as not the answer will be, "Coasting. You?"

The temptation of this coasting time, the two mid-summer months, is for a grower to turn his back on the vineyard for a while, to get up with the sun and not before it. He can be tempted, when his fatigue passes, to move such long-term projects as building maintenance and remodeling to the top of his list and to work on those projects with concentration. That temptation could betray any farmer.

True, the crop has bloomed and set. Vine growth has been thinned and all prudent steps taken to defend against traditional enemies. In this valley, by coasting time, we have made it past frost and killed the weeds, or at least the ones that will die. We have dealt with leafhoppers, mites, grape-eating larvae and the pupating moths called omnivorous leaf rollers. We have cast our chemical spells against mildew and bunch rot. But every year there is the unexpected, and now the unexpected becomes harder to detect. The pace of the year has not stopped, but it has slowed so much and so suddenly, in comparison to the rush of spring just past, that a farmer must look much more closely to see any potentially dangerous change in the vineyard before it becomes a damaging surprise. The changes, too, show much more slowly.

A prudent grape grower wades through the rustling leaves on his vines often, all through summer, praying every time that all he sees will still be green. The central farming secret for this apparently placid time of the year, when the vines have turned inward like brooding mothers, is contained in one dictum: keep your canopy on. The leaves spread like a canopy above each vine are doing it all now, reaching for the sun's energy and turning it into carbohydrates. The carbohydrates not used in ripening go into storage in a healthy vine and are used to start the growing process in the following spring. It is not unusual for a vine that loses its leaf efficiency in any given summer to insect damage or lack of water to not only fail to ripen that year's crop but also to struggle for two or three years afterward before returning to production levels that are normal for its fellows.

So grape farmers stalk their rows like ardent young interns, searching for symptons of trouble in their leaves. They look everywhere for the little grey patches on leaves or spots on grapes that mean mildew has gotten a foothold just there. They look for wilting leaves or cane tips, which tell of a shortage of water so severe in that vine that the plant is puckering up its growing parts. They search for any sign of insect damage: yellow spots left by feeding leafhoppers, red mottling showing a colony of spider mites at work or the dirty bronze scabs left by feeding thrips. The trick is to catch the symptons when first they show and to treat the infection at its start, by washing off the mildew, by spot irrigation or by spraying the feeding insects, before whatever it is that is hurting the leaves has had time to spread.

A grower coasts, but carefully, and there is no convincing reason to relax until a particular moment, usually sometime late in July, when the fat, green berries in their

Above: A mature vine leaf, after irrigation, in perfect condition. The grower's summer chore is to keep all his leaves looking this way.

Left: Crop-dusting airplanes are used most often early in the growing season or near the end, when tractors might damage fully grown vines.

bunches soften one by one. They turn translucent first; then they slowly flush with their natural colors as if each were being filled with wine from within. The pale yellow, the gold, the deep red or the dusty purple color of the wine's soul slowly flowing into green bunches does, finally, bring a sense of relief. For the first time in the year it seems fitting to call the fruit on the vines grapes. These grapes, once they color, are out of reach of some of their enemies and on their way to becoming wine.

A grower must still watch over the vine leaves and worry about the weather at harvest, but several dangers will diminish and fade in the panting days of August coming up. At this moment, when the grapes turn, a grower might be justified in feeling like a river-runner breaking out of a long, dinning stretch of rapids and into a deep, broad reach of the river. The current at work feels smooth and powerful. Natural magic is apparent in the vineyard again. It seems to be taking us all together safely toward a known end.

Well into the summer, red-wine grapes begin to color.

But not in 1980. That year, wine colors began to show in the vineyard at the end of one July week of the kind of California heat that turns the already brown hillside grass into stiff tinder and dries out unirrigated soil until the ground is as hard as an abandoned bone. Such heat, although it leaves people gasping, gets grapes ripe.

Saturday, July 26. Clear. High 95+°. 0600–1200 Miguel, Juan, Ausilio, Mario, Adolfo thin Gamay. Scattered coloring in Gamay.

The ripening heat continued for another week and then vanished for the whole month of August, normally the month with the highest average temperatures of the year.

Monday, August 4. Fog. Cool.

Wednesday, August 6. Fog. Persistent, wet. Bare 80s.

Saturday, August 9. Fog. Drizzle. Slight signs mildew in Carignane.

Thursday, August 14. Fog. Barely 80°. Too cool!

Tuesday, August 19. Fog. Drizzle, then 90°. Bad insect damage.

The fog of that August was not the picturesque white bank that floods through the Golden Gate before sunset and cools off San Francisco on almost every summer afternoon. That fog, the normal fog from the Pacific, burns off the city by ten on most mornings. Our fogs are even milder. The normal summer fog in northern Sonoma County and in Napa County is one of the meteorological reasons why California's great wines are grown and made here. The fog that slips up the river valleys just before dawn and burns off well before noon takes the edge off our hottest days and keeps the acids and sugar in balance inside each grape. It is a winemaker's ally, in the way that cool ocean air is an ally of great wines in the Bordeaux region of France and cool river air in the trough of the Rhone Valley is a friend to Burgundian growers and winemakers.

Friday, August 29. Fog. 80+°. No help. First day sun did not take chill out of air after clearing. Fall?

This fog was no ally. It did not take the edge off our

Left: Each bunch gathers its final color slowly, as though wine were filtering into the bunch grape by grape.

Above: White-wine grapes beginning to ripen and turn soft.

heat; it drew the heat away like a wet, grey-cotton blanket. Between August 4 and September 15 that year, there were only seven scattered days without a dripping fog at sunrise that clung until well after noon. The fog sat on the growing season and on our spirits. Coloring slowed. There was no apparent ripening. Cool-weather pests such as mildew and the speedy, grey insects called thrips returned. Eventually, even bunch rot showed up.

Botrytis cinerea, the most aggressive fungus that haunts vineyards, is usually the leading rotting agent, but plant pathologists can expatiate for hours on the different kinds of molds and fungi that blend to rot grapes near harvest. However, the name bunch rot says everything anyone needs to know. Overnight, the first grey fungus spots meld and spread, like mold over the surface of a cheese. The taut skins of affected grapes collapse as spores feed on the sweet juice within. The juice ferments and drips through cracked skins, carrying more spores with it to neighboring bunches.

Under the right conditions for bunch rot, such as the still calm following an early-season rain or that clinging lukewarm fog in 1980, the stuff can spread in three to five days from a few bunches on a few vines to all the vines covering several acres. Rot-struck bunches turn to unusable mush and literally drip off their vines. Bunch rot is so swift to ruin a crop in certain wine grape varieties that if a grower misses the first signs and returns to that block one week later, he will smell rot at work without even looking, when the sour odor of badly fermenting grapes hits his nose. Rot in a vineyard smells strongly, as though a door to a dirty, abandoned winery had opened under the wines.

All month long and into the early days of September, when harvest would usually be well underway, grape growers to the north of San Francisco sprayed for insects and dusted with fungicides to try to halt bunch rot. Farmers here normally plan family vacations for August. Some grape growers always get away for the August opening of deer season. Not in 1980.

Every gloomy day of temperatures between 75 and 85 degrees brought us nearer to the rainy end of the growing season with no ripening heat. Farmers' dispositions grew as dingy as the weather. In the second week of September, a cheerful local winemaker with a loud voice and a long list of suppliers among local growers was commiserating one afternoon with some of those he knew.

"If this keeps up," he said of the weather, "there may be some varieties out there that won't get ripe at all."

No one spoke. He looked around at us in the silence.

"Sorry," he said in a quiet tone.

And in my help house during that gloomy August, Ausilio Torres went for morose days on end without working. He did not join the others who had signed up with another farmer to clear land for a new vineyard. That is a job requiring extra hands, and it is normally done just before harvest, when work in established vineyards like mine is slack.

Ausilio barely spoke to me, but he apparently drove the Silva brothers to distraction by handling them with an uncle's discipline when they came home. He required almost nightly that they serve as chauffeur and escort, driving him into town and waiting as he made his drinking visits. He goaded them, I saw in the course of one incident, as though he resented them being alive when his son was dead.

Privately, and as obliquely as Latin tact requires, I tried to suggest to Ausilio that Humberto might not have wanted his father to remember him by drinking and that the living deserved some consideration. The gentle, friendly man who had been like an uncle to everyone in my field crews in the past said nothing in particular. Two days later he moved off the place without notice. The embarrassed young men could not or would not say where Ausilio had gone. We all went our separate ways in the fog.

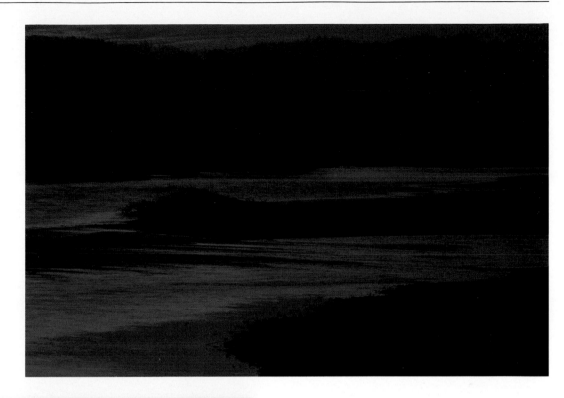

Above: Rivers and creeks drop to slow-moving summer levels.

Left: Summer fog moves off the ocean and inland over the coast north of San Francisco. When it burns off the vineyards in the morning, fog is a winemaker's ally. If it holds on, it delays ripening.

CHAPTER NINE

Harvest

The harvest is the known end of the vineyard year, anticipated with certainty from the day the grapes were born. It clicks closer with every hot summer day, and its precise and proper start in any wine vineyard can be determined with instruments; yet the first day of picking seems always to pounce.

The North Coast vineyard region seems to anticipate harvest in somewhat the way many Californians anticipate the next great earthquake. Everyone in wine county knows that harvest is coming and all are in some way prepared, but none of us, not growers, winemakers, truckers or pickers, ever seem fully ready for the first rattled day of the turmoil that follows. From early August on, every grape grower in California knows it pays to clean and paint his harvest bins and tanks, to tune up his trucks and overhaul special harvest equipment, to be ready, in short, at any time. Yet I have found myself wrestling slippery hydraulic

Hop kiln, a monument to another farming era.

hoses onto their connections in a harvest loader by flashlight on the night before the pickers were due to start, and other, more experienced growers have borrowed equipment from me in the middle of it all. We all do it. We get as ready as we can, but when the surprises and the breakdowns come, we do the fastest thing that comes to hand to keep going. Once picking starts, the only thing that counts in grape growing is "getting it off," to use the local phrase, but the relief found in the first day of getting the crop off may sometimes be postponed by nature.

Growers have ridden the current of a year almost to its familiar finish by September; then the flow seems to check. Mature grapes sit without change under mature leaves while ripeness builds slowly inside. There is a tense and worrisome pause during which nothing can be done. When, finally, a farmer's grapes are ripe enough to make wine, it is as though a natural dam has burst, and the harvest sweeps

Above: Slow-starting harvest
under grey skies.

Right: Grapes struggling to
ripen in a cool summer.

every other consideration out of its way. Winemakers call harvest "the crush," a name that fits not only what they do to ripe wine grapes, but also the way they must often feel, once that dam has truly burst.

In the cool, grey 1980 season, however, it held and held. The largest winery in Sonoma County, a wholly owned subsidiary of the giant Gallo organization, which buys and crushes half of all the wine grapes grown in Sonoma and Mendocino counties, opened on September 4 that year under a drizzle. And the fog held on for a week. On any given day, there seemed to be more employees than there were grape trucks on the cement pad around the stainless-steel crushing machinery. They walked through the winery's forest of four-story stainless tanks with nothing to do. Well into September, when the place should have been full of the deep hum of the crushing machinery, the whine of transfer pumps, the noise of truck and tractor motors and the reverberating rumble that comes from a 50,000-gallon tank when wine first starts to pour into it, that winery was empty and echoing.

September is normally our most favored month. It is the month, the records show, of San Francisco's rare heat waves, when daytime highs reach their highest. Those records point to another of the natural blessings that have made Sonoma, Napa and Mendocino counties the most favored ground for California's premium wine vineyards. The ocean fog bank recedes from the California coast in September. The northwest winds from the cold Pacific die. San Franciscans call it Indian summer and swelter at 87 degrees. In wine country, we make it out to be ripening weather, and we hang on its return.

A September heat wave can save a bad year, when the huge mountain of air called the semipermanent mid-Pacific high slides inland off a glassy ocean and over our coastal valleys like a vast greenhouse roof. The high pressure blocks the storms brewing to its west, and the temperature in the vineyards climbs and holds, day after cloudless, windless day. Grapes that have not ripened fill steadily with sugar. The sun rises through a red haze of yesterday's dust

trapped on the horizon and presses down on us all day. Bees dance in a purposeful, rippling frieze of golden dots above each full tank of grapes, and heat rises in visible waves off trucks and tractors. Dust trails moving equipment everywhere. Grape pickers gasp and even the toughest flag early in the afternoon. On such days a Dry Creek First-Aid Kit: two bags of ice and a case of beer in a carton, rushed into the rows for the picking crew, can keep everyone going toward the goal of getting the crop off fast.

The reasons we push hardest in the heat is sharp and simple. Grapes rise to their perfect peak, the winemaker's dream of perfection, only once at the end of their lives. In a September heat wave, wine grapes peak fast and are gone past perfection within a few days or a week. An Indian summer harvest is hard and fast, because since 1977 all North Coast wineries have steadily narrowed their definitions of topmost quality, expressed in terms of maximum and minimum levels of sugar in the grapes. The best price is paid for grapes that exactly fit the winery's established optimum; therefore it pays to know precisely when to pick and to strip the vines as fast as men and machines can manage it.

Friday, September 12. Fog. 80°. 0800–1530 Woodpile with Ausilio and son. A.M. Captan dust Zins to oak tree, every row, 40# per acre for rot. 1700 WIND CHANGE N! WEATHER CHANGE COMING.

The effect of that late-afternoon wind shift was like that of bugles or bagpipes. That north wind, in the fall, is pouring off the edge of the Pacific high as it begins its ponderous move eastward out of the way of winter. The wind is like the draft through a huge, slowly opening door, and it means that Indian summer is not far behind. It blows away the fog and it says to the grower as loudly as bugles: get ready now. Equipment? Check. Truck? Check. Grape knives? Check. Picking tubs? Check. Pickers? Where were the pickers who had been driving into the shop or the barnyard for two gloomy weeks or more, looking for work that could not yet be done? My God, could they all have given up and gone away?

It turned out that they had not. In fact, three days

A picker eats grapes to get a
quick boost of energy.

A Vineyard Year

before that late-afternoon wind shift, Ausilio Torres had returned without a word, bringing his youngest son, Rene, with him. The Silva brothers said nothing. It happened that one day Ausilio was not there and the next day he was. I sensed that there had been some form of reconciliation and let it go at that, in large part because the best way I have found to be reasonably sure of signing on a congenial picking crew is to be sure the resident hands, with whom a grower already gets along, know and approve of the men or families who come to work only for the grape harvest. Miguel, I remembered, had attracted two good crews to the place one year earlier, and before that, Ausilio had always been unobtrusively good at smoothing out rough spots in harvest labor relations.

When Miguel and Ausilio together introduced the Chavez brothers, broad men both with flat, black eyes and high cheekbones, and their four somewhat motley traveling companions, I paid little attention to subtleties. The north wind was blowing. I needed pickers. I opened and cleaned the harvest bunkhouse, connected water and gas and assigned it to the Chavez party. That gesture has an almost contractual significance for seasonal laborers. It is understood by all that if a grower supplies quarters to help hired for harvest, those living on his place are committed to pick with him whenever he picks and can work elsewhere only when he is not harvesting. By housing the Chavez brothers and their followers, I had filled half my basic picking crew. The rest would come from outside the vineyard, from among migrant bachelors who follow the harvests up and down the West Coast and from resident families who work together in the vineyards once a year.

We were ready, but still the grapes were not. Beginning late in August, in most years, a grower starts almost unconsciously to test the readiness of his grapes between thumb and forefinger as he walks through a vineyard on his rounds. When they feel soft to the pinch and are fully colored, he will start testing with his mouth by picking one grape off a bunch at random and tasting it. At first the grapes are sour enough to make a pig squeal, which is fine, because

Pablo and Carmen Cazarez, year-round vineyard workers, enlist their three daughters for the seasonal work of picking grapes near Livermore.

Above and opposite: The sun heats the coastal valleys to over 100 degrees. Men, women and machines work as fast as they can force themselves and each other in the superheated dust.

Right: Adolfina Pardo.

the wild pigs that haunt our hills in herds descended from domesticated boars and sows that broke out of farm pens long ago are very discerning. They will not attempt to eat grapes from the vine until those grapes have sweetened to above 18 degrees on the scale, called Brix or Balling, used throughout the wine business to gauge the sugar content of wine grapes. Eighteen degrees on that scale translates into a grape sweet enough for humans—and wild pigs—to eat with relish. That point is the ideal one for grapes grown for the table, but grapes for all but champagne must be much riper.

When wine grapes are barely ready for the crusher and fermenter, at 21 or 22 degrees Brix, they taste oversweet, almost cloying. Winemakers prefer white grapes for most white wines at 22 degrees, and they would like all the grapes that farmers call "blacks," for all red wines, to be slightly above 23 degrees when they are tipped into the crusher. Each degree between 18 and 22 may not be clear in every grower's mouth, but the oversweet taste of full ripeness is unmistakable to most, as unmistakable as the first piece cut from a cake made by a cook who has inadvertently doubled the sugar measure.

Near the end, it is always best to test for sugar content with instruments. The technique is simple. A grower picks a bucketful of grapes on a cross-sectioning walk through the vineyard and crushes them. He stirs up the juice and puts a few drops on the prismatic tip of an instrument called a hand-held refractometer. The way sunlight bends through the film of grape juice on the tip is translated into a black shadow across an eyepiece at the other end of the instrument. Where the black shadow falls across an internally inscribed scale, it marks the degree of sweetness in the grapes being tested. Normally, growers use refractometers when close to picking to determine the best possible moment to start. That September, we found ourselves using them to see how far away the harvest might be. The black shadow fell far short of normal levels.

Friday, September 19. Fog. 0930–1600 Miguel, Juan wire brush on Dry Creek bank. Half-hour lunch. Help hill test scant 20 degrees! Zins on flat 21.

Above: Dolores Martinez.

Right: Loading grapes.

By the same date one year earlier, the block we call the help hill had been picked and delivered at 23.2, and the block of Zinfandel vines on the flat valley floor tested 23.4 degrees. One year later, the hill block would be picked by September 1.

The 1980 weather stayed cool but windy. Bunch rot, where it had started, stopped spreading and dried up. Still the ripening dragged. On September 20, the white French Colombard grapes in our vineyard tested at 20 degrees Brix. On the same day one year earlier, that same block had tested at 23 while we were picking through it. One year later, we were to finish picking the Colombard by September 4. However, there was one sign of hope in the sky: the moon, waxing toward full on September 24. Weather changes often come with changes in the moon.

> Sunday, September 21. Clear. Still 85+°. No help. Indian summer? Hot all day.

> Monday, September 22. Clear. 90+°. Indian summer indeed. Clear picking avenues. Tanks on. House hill test 22.5, cemetery hill 22.5.

The high moved ashore on Monday, two days before the moon began to wane. The temperature climbed and held. The 1980 harvest was on.

Suddenly that week, almost every variety of wine grape grown in the county seemed to get ripe at once. Trucks carrying loads of normally early-maturing white grapes lined up at all wineries, three weeks later than usual, with trucks carrying grapes for red wines such as Zinfandel, which were then slightly overdue, and even Cabernet Sauvignon, which normally would not start coming in until October. The lines of trucks waiting their turn at the crushers grew, and the growers waiting for them stewed, knowing that almost everything they had on the vine would have to come off practically at once. We all were reminded over and over again, by what was happening, of the flat judgment reached after thirty years in the business by the chief winemaker of the largest winery in the state, who said then and still says, "There is no normal year."

It seems to me, though, that there is a normal first day for every grape harvest. The pickers gather at first light, as eager and as edgy as runners waiting for a marathon to start. Some chatter, stretch and walk about. Others sit alone. Impatiently, when the grower is ready, they give their names and social security numbers. Quickly, they trot into the vineyard as soon as they know where the picking is to begin. On that first morning, they will shout at a grower in a rage if they must wait for empty bins or gondolas into which to empty their full picking tubs. They will sing suddenly or shout across the rows.

"Oye, Juan," comes a disembodied voice from among the yellow and red leaves halfway across the hill. "Juan, you'd better hurry up and pick or we'll have to send the widow lady to help you get out by lunchtime."

"Save her," Juan shouts back, never stopping the rhythm with which he is cutting the purple bunches off and letting them drop into his plastic tub under that vine. "With all the beer you drink, you'll need her to carry you home."

A grower is hard put to keep up at first. The mechanical rhythm of moving full containers out of the vineyard and empty containers in does not come back immediately

Late-summer view of a hill vineyard waiting for harvest.

to tractor or man. There are little breakdowns and slippages in the equipment. But, by midday, the pace settles and the mood for all turns silent and earnest. Almost unexpectedly a grower has the first load of the year, grapes piled high in a steel tank, with one side sloped for dumping and a hinge on the same side, bolted to the rail of the truck's flat bed or riding its own trailer in and out of the vineyard and over the road to the winery.

The ride to the winery is a commonplace. A grower has done it a hundred times before. And yet, there are four or eight or ten or even twenty-four tons' worth of one year of his life riding behind him on the way. At an open-sided shack on stilts alongside the winery entrance, he will be judged.

A grower drives up to that shack. Stops with his grapes smiling up at the men standing on its open platform. Sets his brake and climbs down. Climbs up the steps to the same level as his grapes. Punching deep into the heaped bunches with four-foot stainless-steel tubes, four inches wide at their sharp mouths, the men in the sugar shack will already be coring his load, dumping their sampling of his life into the stained hopper above a grinding grape press. The grinder motor whirs. The grape juice runs free into a once-white bucket. The tester mixes it with a practiced swirl, dips in a refractometer like the grower's and asks, "Variety?"

"Zinfandel," the grower replies. It is all very clipped and cool. With the refractometer to one eye, the tester closes the other and squints through the instrument into the westering sun.

"23.2."

"Thanks."

The grower gets down the steps with his precious sugar slip now in hand, clamping his jaw muscles down on a smile. The minimum sugar content required is 22 degrees Brix. The winery has said it will pay a bonus for every tenth of a degree above 22 up to 23.5. Pretty close to perfect, that one was. Would that they all could be.

If the sugar is right on that first load, the rest of the first-day ritual is a routine relief for a grower. He weighs in at the scale. Waits. Wheels in, when his turn comes, under the hoist by the crusher. Watches the grapes slide out like a purple cascade into the stainless-steel trough where an end-less stainless screw spins. The winery hoist lifts the free side of his tank up past the perpendicular. The grapes slump out over the sloping tank side with a whuffing sound. They cover the crushing screw and heave and ripple above it. After one year away, he's home again.

On the way out he should be a different man, seasoned, a veteran heading back into the front lines at a confident pace. He stops again at the scale, for the difference between his truck weight in and empty weight out equals the grapes he has delivered. It is the first increment of his once-yearly paycheck.

Usually, a man can wave casually at those still in the sugar shack as he accelerates past it on the way back to the grapes that have just made him proud.

So it went, exactly, on September 27 of that long-drawn-out and suddenly reprieved growing season of 1980. On my place, we picked the red-wine grapes off the dry hills first, then worked through the French Colombard. The tons piled up and the sugars climbed. Work went ahead from first light until after dark every day but Sunday, when the wineries close and everyone gets a chance to fix whatever broke and was patched during the week. I later calculated that my picking crews, paid for each half-ton bin filled in the field, were earning just under seven dollars for each hour they had spent running among the vines, hoisting their filled tubs and trotting them to a bin, then loping back to the next vine.

There was a hugely happy feeling abroad throughout the Dry Creek Valley. No one had time to stop and gloat, but the gloom had gone with the fog. The pickers were making money fast. The growers were getting their crops off, and the grapes were rolling steadily into the wineries with very high quality forged in that cool August, which had held the wines' taste inside the grapes on each vine, and in the heat that had finally brought the sugar up for strength in the bottle. The year, it seemed, was saved.

Above: Trucks backed up at a winery.

Left: When harvest is late, growers watch the moon because weather changes seem to follow a full moon.

Working from first light to
sunset to get the grapes in.

A Vineyard Year

On Thursday, October 2, as I waited to deliver my second twelve-ton load of white grapes of the day at the Gallo-owned winery, I saw the winemaker in charge. Sweat stood out from his forehead in the 100-degree heat, but he was ecstatic.

"We just got a lab test you would not believe," he said. "Tank 306 will be a legend. It's Cabernet at 25 degrees Brix, 1 percent of titratable acids and a 3.2 pH. It's out of the textbooks."

I pulled my truck ahead and smiled at the retired farmer who had helped out during harvest at that winery for years before Gallo Vineyards bought and remade it, before the ecstatic winemaker had come.

"We needed this heat two months ago," the farmer said as we watched the grapes spill out of my tank and into the rumbling crusher. "And we need the fog we had then, now. You watch."

The retired farmer was right. Gallo's winemaker had just watched that season's peak go past. Indian summer had lasted too long, and already many of those red-wine grapes as yet unpicked, for lack of time, had started to pucker, to shrivel on the vine.

On the next day Julio Gallo himself, the patriarch of the organization, came to inspect the grapes his winery here was taking in. Gallo's visits are not unusual. He drops out of the sky over Dry Creek Valley in his green-and-white helicopter and onto the landing pad of his winery perhaps once a week and sometimes more often during the crush. Gallo has a reputation as one of the most knowledgeable wine men in the world, but no local grower wants to be the one on whom he proves that reputation during any visit. Therefore, those of us in Dry Creek Valley who can see the helicopter fly in normally avoid delivering until we see it fly out. Growers from the Alexander Valley, the lower Russian River or Mendocino County, because they cannot see him come, are usually the ones to pass under Julio Gallo's eye. That October 3 I was already at the end of the line of trucks waiting for their sugar tests when the helicopter settled onto its well-tended grass landing pad. When Gallo started walk-

A season saved by the weather makes everyone in the wine business happy.

ing up the line, climbing onto the first waiting trucks and judging the grapes in them, there was no turning back.

Like a distant spectator at a coronation or a coup d'état, I saw only small figures, a few gestures and some blurred scurrying. Gallo never reached the end of the line that day, but a few trucks where he had been began to back and turn, to leave without unloading. The word came back along the line of trucks that Gallo himself had turned them away, rejecting outright the grapes in those loads. The rest of us crept our trucks forward in their lowest and slowest gears. A vineyard manager I knew rode out from the head of the line in the cab of a double-trailer rig carrying twenty-four tons of white grapes. Here and there in those grapes, which were back-lit by the sun as he drove past, we all could see

**Above: Grape pickers
move from vine to vine at
a quick trot.**

**Right: A picker empties his full
tub into a half-ton bin.**

Above: The moment of truth. Testers at the winery sugar shack take a sample that will determine what price a load of grapes will command.

Right: First load of the season. Frank Teldeschi, of the Dry Creek Valley Teldeschis, heads to the winery towing grapes in a steel trailer, called a gondola, behind his tractor.

the grey blotches of bunch rot. The grower's face was the same color.

Right there, in the forenoon sun of the fifth 100-degree day in row, the rules for the harvest changed. The joint elation of the growers and winemakers in the country over a whole crop saved by the weather disappeared, and we became antagonists. We all had known there was bunch rot in the vineyards. That was the work of the foggy weather. We all had begun to see withering in the grapes still unpicked. That was the work of the heat that had followed the fog.

In the preceding ten years of the wine grape boom, independent growers and the wineries that bought their grapes together had accepted such fluctuations in quality as the work of natural forces, the kind of act of God against which no one is expected to insure. The grower, in those years, had been expected to do his best by picking and hauling only his healthiest grapes. The wineries, for their part under those flexible unwritten rules, had overlooked some defects on some bunches, so long as there were not too many in any one load.

After the Friday of Julio Gallo's inspection in the October heat, the unwritten rules suddenly changed. Every load going to his winery was inspected by an experienced winemaker. The inspector rejected the load, or accepted it with an A or a B grade. After a day under the new procedure, we learned that a B grade meant that the load would be paid for at some price below the established price for that variety of grapes, whatever the established price might later turn out to be. Those were the rules. Take it or, as one heard more and more often in the days that followed, take your grapes down the road.

The shock was total and largely private. A man would no more approach one of his neighbors who was stomping back to his truck with his face flaming, or sitting on the running board and staring into space after the inspector moved on, than he would ask the same neighbor what the doctor had said if he knew the man were waiting for the results of his wife's biopsy. The new procedure, growers

First day's picking. The load tumbles out of the tank and into the crusher.

Right: Bunch rot has just begun to show in the white-wine grapes, in the form of split skins and a greyish color inside a few crumpled grapes.

discovered quietly, was legal. And those who tried to sell elsewhere loads rejected at the Gallo winery found the same rules applied everywhere.

There was no conspiracy. Although we did not wholly grasp it then, we all had passed a turning point in the history of the California wine industry. The supply of wine grapes had caught up with the new American thirst for wine. From that moment in that harvest on, almost anywhere in California, but most particularly here on the North Coast, where the wines that made California famous are grown, only the best grapes would be bought at full price. Take it, the word went, or take your grapes down the road. But there was no other winery down the road. Throughout Sonoma and Napa counties, the wineries wanted just what they wanted and nothing more, and that was all a grower could deliver. A man did what he had to do.

The two grown sons of a second-generation Italian wine-grape farmer in the Dry Creek Valley quietly drove their one rejected load home and parked their truck on the creek bank. Standing together in their grapes, they shoveled six tons out onto the ground. There is no other way to unload grapes that will not be made into wine. They finished as the moon was setting and did not tell anyone outside the family what they had had to do until months later.

In the superheated vineyards, farmers called out their wives, their mothers, retired or urban relatives, anyone who could tell good grapes from bad. Then, while the grower made sure his pickers did not cut wholly rotten or wholly dry bunches, his relatives stood sorting at the bins or the truck, clipping out partial corners of rotten or withered grapes and leaving them on the ground. Wherever grape trucks were being loaded in the valley, an aureole of discarded grapes lay in the dust.

Grape pickers everywhere rebelled at the sudden change in standards. Their harvest earnings depend on being able to cut a lot of weight off the vines with their hooked picking knives quickly and without having to move too much to fill one tub. Two forty-pound tubs from one vine is considered fine picking, but if a picker has to select

Red-wine grapes that have raisined on the vine will not make wine.

only some bunches from four vines or more to fill one tub, his or her earnings drop drastically. Understandably, there were strikes or walkouts in almost every vineyard.

Mine came on the morning of October 8, when the Chavez brothers drove off and brought back a case of beer. With Miguel, Juan and their four followers, they sat down to drink in the shade and picked no more. The outside pickers simply left. Only Ausilio and his son Rene went on selecting the best grapes left on those vines, cutting them and carrying them out. I picked with them into the afternoon, and we hauled three tons to the winery that day. The two Torres men had picked almost half of the load.

The only way to relieve the antagonism and continue getting the crop off was to renegotiate the price paid for each container picked. Everywhere pickers returned to work, usually for at least 25 percent more for each ton picked, because they found the same grim rules in every vineyard. Adaptation followed resignation, from the wineries back into the vineyards and on to the men and women picking that crop. The antagonism might be resolved but the tension held on. The harvest had soured. It turned into an endurance test.

At the winery, the wait to unload grew from one hour to four. At first, by turning over the hauling to a hired driver, a relative or a friend during the day, growers found they could pick the same tonnage on each sweltering day by waiting in line with the last load well into the night. It was worth it to try to stay ahead of the shriveling heat. Heat-dried grapes could mean a rejected or downgraded load. Then the overflowing wineries imposed daily delivery quotas. The amount any grower could harvest was cut in half by some quotas, and the grapes went on drying out.

When grapes pass their peak too fast in the harvest season, each picker's tub must be inspected to make sure no rotting or dried grapes get in the load going to the winery.

When dehydration strikes a vineyard, the rule of thumb derived from laboratory studies is: once the surface of the grape puckers visibly, 30 percent of its weight is gone. As that Indian summer wore on into its third week, we discarded grapes that looked like raisins by the bunchful and prayed that some puckered skins on other bunches would pass the inspector. Some varieties held up well in the heat, but with others at least one-third of the crop by weight already had been lost by the time the pickers reached them.

So far as anyone could tell, the anger initially felt by farmers caught in that year's double bind between weather that dried out grapes and wineries that would not accept dried grapes, but also would not allow a full day's picking, wore off quickly during the long, hot waits in line. Men wandered from truck to truck exchanging news, rumors and cold cans of beer, and their attitudes changed with every day they had made it through. Almost all grew to like the chief inspector at the Gallo-owned winery here. He knew his business, the waiting farmers said, and his job was not his fault. The latter half of their judgment seemed to imply that inspection had become just another force of nature, to be accepted the way a grower accepts wind during bloom or heat at harvest. Nothing a man can do to change those. But floating through the gripes and the gossip exchanged during those conversations in line, there were reflections on grape growing as a business. Men were rethinking their plans.

I wrote down in my field log one grower's judgment that "This valley will all be houses if this keeps up."

"I had been planning to buy more acreage," said another on another day. "But I surely won't now."

Finally the heat was broken, late on October 11, by a line of thunderstorms that swirled in from the south under the skirt of the high pressure sitting over us. Rain pelted down on the last trucks in line on that Saturday night when the front arrived.

"Good night," said a sixty-seven-year-old farmer as he drove off the crusher pad that evening. "We're through for the year, and you know, I'm going to go get that social security next year. Enough of this for me."

Exactly one week later, I finished picking too.

Sunday, October 19. Done. Went to Mass. 301 tons total. Bonus due on Zins and Carignane.

The growing season is not always completely finished when the picking is done. The rush ends, but the grape grower drifts on slowly, like a leaf in a stream, and slowly the warmth goes out of what is left of the year. Our vineyards, after picking, look tattered and forlorn, as though they had been roughed up and abandoned in the fields. Without a frost or heavy rains, the vines slip gently into dormancy. Their leaves grow brittle to the touch without dropping. In the silence following harvest, if it does not rain, there are chores to be done: ripping up the ground compacted by tractors all year to leave it open for the winter rain and allow roots to grow again, applying certain kinds of fertilizer, clearing away the harvest equipment, putting together a barbecue for the picking crews.

The great gold harvest moon swings past and the first frost touches down. One day starlings return, on their way south. In huge, whirring flocks they scour the valley for days, gleaning the vineyards. They chirp and chatter, with a noise like a distant crowd of schoolchilden, only when they are roosting or feeding. The chirping stops abruptly when the birds rise as a flock. In the silence that follows, their myriad whirring wings make a sound like a muffled explosion. In the air, the flocks turn like black smoke in a wind, forming fantastic patterns. The starlings seem to follow no one leader for more than a moment; so the hundreds of thousands of black birds swirl overhead, shaping the flock into patterns that flow into one another across the sky. Thunderheads become tornadoes that change into bears that disappear into waterfalls as the birds land.

As the sun gets lower on the southern horizon every day, there comes a certain light, late in the afternoon, in which a turning flock of starlings, banking all together with their million wings on end, disappears.

It is time to start pruning again.

Post-harvest detail in red-wine grape vineyards.

Indian summer harvest — the desperate phase.

Ausilio Torres, left, the Chavez
brothers and their friends open
a "Dry Creek First Aid Kit"
after a day's picking in the heat.

White-wine grapevines stand,
clean and harvested, their
leaves dying slowly as the
vines drift into dormancy.

A Vineyard Year

Indian summer heat normally breaks at the first rainy touch of the California winter.

A Vineyard Year

The vintage of 1980 is in the bottle now, and on the balance sheets kept by wine grape growers. The wines made that September and October taste much better than the economic realities that growers have faced, beginning then. That year's wines, at least, hold fine memories of the way things once were.

Remembering the long, cool summer of 1980 and the sudden heat at harvest, any California winemaker or grower would expect the early-maturing white grapes, picked before the heat began, to have produced the best wines of that year. Pinot Chardonnay and Johannisberg Riesling, for example, were pretty certain bets to have matured quietly in the cool summer, as they do in northeastern France and the Rhine Valley, and to have made exceptional wines in 1980. Early harvest red-wine grapes, notably Gamay Beaujolais, would almost certainly have escaped the withering heat of Indian summer that October. Since they are picked early every year, Gamay Beaujolais and its cousin, Pinot Noir, should have more flavor in most bottles dated 1980 than those from northern California in more conventional vineyard years. That kind of wine country expectation for the wines of 1980 has largely been fulfilled.

Gold medals at the top two California competitive tastings—the Orange County Fair and the Los Angeles County Fair—have been awarded to three Chardonnays from this northern corner of Sonoma County: Chateau St. Jean (R. Young Vineyards), Dry Creek Vineyards Vintner's Reserve and Alexander Valley Vineyards. Alexander Valley Vineyards and Chateau St. Jean also received medals for 1980 Johannisberg Rieslings.

Among the early red wines grown and bottled here that year, the Mill Creek Vineyards Merlot (Dry Creek Valley) has won a gold medal at the Los Angeles County Fair, J. Pedroncelli's Gamay Beaujolais has won four medals and A. Rafanelli's 1980 Gamay Beaujolais may be one of the best he has bottled. The local wines that we all expected to turn out well have been at the very top in competitive tastings in the state and on a national scale, but the same tastings have revealed some surprises.

Late-maturing white grapes—the Gewürztraminers and Sauvignon Blancs—have done very well at the statewide tastings also, notably the Chateau St. Jean (Frank Johnson Vineyards) Gewürztraminer and the Sauvignon Blanc wines bottled that year by Dry Creek Vineyards, Preston Vineyards and Foppiano Winery. And some of the midseason red-wine grapes have appeared recently as winners too— even Zinfandels. There is a lesson in local knowledge hidden in these results, and it can be passed along. The lesson lies in the fact that the prize-winning wines were made at relatively small wineries.

The grapes for all of our deep-flavored red wines—Zinfandel, Petite Sirah and even Cabernet Sauvignon—were either harvested as the heat first hit, and therefore at their only peak, or after the October heat wave had hung on too long. The memory of that difference in timing will almost certainly show up in the taste of the wines in their bottles. The best bets for that year's reds, then, will be found in the small and medium-scale wineries, which got their crops off in time to make the best wine and did not mix in grapes that had withered or partially dried. Such grapes leave a very slight taste of burnt sugar in the mouth, like that of a delicately made caramel custard. So, when looking for Zinfandel wines from 1980, this grower will go to A. Rafanelli Winery, not just because it is next door, but because I know Americo Rafanelli got his Zinfandel off before it ripened too far. I would count on Lou Preston, at Preston Vineyards, to have done the same, as well as the Demosthene brothers at Sausal Winery. But these are my usual favorites.

A grower's general advice to anyone interested in the big red wines of 1980 would be to stick to wineries producing about 50,000 cases annually, because they were not overwhelmed by the radical changes in weather that year. I also suspect that some of the 1980 Cabernet Sauvignon, when it is finally released, is going to be among the best ever made in California. Even Napa Gamay, the latest-maturing of all the red-wine grapes, made extraordinarily good wine that year, and that is a good sign. We will all know if I am right by 1985.

There were a number of other happy endings in 1980. Shortly after harvest, Ausilio Torres stopped drinking away the memory of his son Humberto's death. He and his son Rene have returned to Mexico and are reported to be happily farming their own land, and that of several neighbors, with the tractor and the truck Ausilio and his first-born son had taken home years earlier. Miguel and Juan Silva pruned with me into 1981, then set off traveling and worked their way into Florida and back before returning to northern California. Their savings, sent home regularly since they first started to work in my vineyard, have built and furnished a solid brick house for their parents. The brothers live in a town apartment and had found eight-to-four-thirty jobs outside the vineyards "for five dollars an hour, finally," Miguel reported to me with pride in the spring of 1983.

Five dollars an hour were my wages for running another grower's harvest crew in 1982, two years after the economic lessons of 1980 took hold. As they did, I sold out. The boom in wine grape production ended in 1980, and with it any reasonable expectation that a grape grower with a mortgage could hope to survive without outside help. Mortgage-free growers and those who can afford to farm for tax losses have been hunkering down all around me to weather some lean years. One can see it in the details of fertilizations foregone and the number of hours a friend, who once might have paid a mechanic to do it, will spend rebuilding his own truck motor. "Once these wineries would take every grape you could grow, and bend down to kiss you good-bye as you left," a very experienced farmer told me in 1980. "Now they are going to take only what they want, exactly as much as they want and nothing more." That has turned out to be exactly true in California. And, although the new rules of the state's wine grape marketplace may be grim news for grape growers, they should mean nothing but benefits for those who buy wine. Wineries have begun paying less for winegrapes, and taking only the best available grapes at their lower prices. They have also begun competing hard for shelf space with each other and with wines imported from Italy and France. The end result for wine drinkers could soon be a mild bonanza of better wines for lower prices. And for the grape grower?

"Perhaps the biggest problem facing grape growers in 1983," Keith Bowers, the highly respected extension-service farm advisor for Napa County wrote in his January 1983 newsletter to the farmers he advises, "and for the next several years will not be pest and disease control or the weather, but the economic problems of growing and selling at a profit."

That is the romance of farming.

INDEX

This book was designed by
Carol Hoover and Howard Jacobsen
of Triad, Fairfax, California.
The text types are Caslon 540 and
Janson bold, set at Type by Design, Fairfax.
The title display is hand-modified American Caslon Italic.
Production assistants were Michael Fennelly, design,
Sara Schrom and John Greenslade, typography,
and Mark Shepard, mechanical production.
Color separations, halftones, printing,
and binding were executed by
Toppan Printing, Co., Ltd.,
Tokyo, Japan.